What People Are S

Pantheon - The

I was excited to read this book, and it did not disappoint. The names of the Roman deities are so familiar that we may think we know all about them, but even for those of us who already have some knowledge, they have many aspects and stories still to explore. In addition to the twenty principal deities of Rome, the author shares the intriguing tales of many lesser-known deities. This information is framed by the unique history of Rome and an exploration of the way Roman religion was intertwined with politics and daily life. All this, combined with the author's insightful advice for beginning a spiritual practice that honors the Roman deities, makes for a valuable reference the reader will return to again and again.

Laura Perry, founder of Ariadne's Tribe and author of *Pantheon - The Minoans*

This interesting overview of Rome blends history with religion and mysticism as it was understood then, creating an intriguing picture that will appeal to admirers of history and mythology alike. The author gives a useful mythological timeline (which appeals to the storyteller in me) and blends in all sorts of details about deities and spirits that I did not previously know. The section on ritual provides a lot of food for thought and will prove useful to anyone wanting to develop a contemporary practice with the Di Consentes and other entities. The calendrical section is ideal in this regard, providing enough information to spark interest and lead to further research. A large portion of the readership will probably want guidance on spirituality

today rather than simply having a purely intellectual interest in Roman history, so this part of the book is especially useful.
Robin Herne, author of *Pantheon - The Egyptians*

The Roman Empire lasted for around 1480 years and had a powerful influence in shaping the lands and the peoples they conquered. Western Europe, North Africa, and those they traded with would never be the same again. In modern-day their influence still lives on in architecture, art, language, and culture, and things people take for granted like roads, sanitation, a counting system, and currency. The power of the empire was possible because the people were unified behind Rome and the Gods that dominated their everyday lives. The author takes the reader through the core of Roman religion and the primary Gods and spirits that influenced the empire with a look at the historical beginnings and how Rome evolved. Although this is a small book it is a valuable addition to anyone who wishes to study this tradition, enabling them to expand their research with the resources she provides. She gives a commentary on the primary Gods/Goddesses and spirits that were worshipped and ways how to introduce them into the life of the reader in order to connect with them on a personal level, incorporating what the Roman people would have used for offerings, decorating personal and household altars, and ritual dress. It is a great guide for the beginner, or a reference guide to have to hand and I look forward to further work from Rachel Sarah on the subject.
Martha Gray, author of *Grimalkyn: The Witch's Cat and Nine's a Charm*

Pantheon
The Romans

Rachel Roberts

Previous Books

Pagan Portals – Lupa

She-Wolf of Rome, Mother of Destiny

978-1-80341-350-1 (Paperback)

978-1-80341-351-8 (e-book)

Wolf; Untamed. Courageous. Empowered

An Inspirational Guide to Embodying Your Inner Wolf

978-1-80341-533-8 (Paperback)

978-1-80341-570-3 (e-book)

This book is dedicated to all history teachers but in particular Mr Dave Healey, or 'Sir' as I still and will always respectfully call you! This book is for you as a thank you, for both your support and inspiration as the best history teacher one could hope for! I will never forget dying from the plague in high school, nor your encouragement of my fascination for the past and bringing history to life. I believe it is important to honour all those that have been influential on our path and for making history fun, interesting, relevant and alive, I will always be grateful to you.

This book is offered in the greatest devotion to Jupiter and Juno, for your guardianship and guidance in its creation. May it serve you well.

First among cities, the home of gods, is golden Rome.
Ausonius, *The Order of Famous Cities*

Pantheon
The Romans

Rachel Roberts

**MOON
BOOKS**
London, UK
Washington, DC, USA

CollectiveInk

First published by Moon Books, 2026
Moon Books is an imprint of Collective Ink Ltd.,
Unit 11, Shepperton House, 89 Shepperton Road, London, N1 3DF
office@collectiveinkbooks.com
www.collectiveinkbooks.com
www.moon-books.net

For distributor details and how to order please visit the 'Ordering' section on our website.

ISBN: 978 1 80341 682 3
978 1 80341 930 5 (ebook)
Library of Congress Control Number: 2024943338

A CIP catalogue record for this book is available from the British Library.

Design: Lapiz Digital Services
Illustrated by Kay Savage

UK: Printed and bound by CPI Group (UK) Ltd, Croydon, CR0 4YY
US: Printed and bound by Thomson-Shore, 7300 West Joy Road, Dexter, MI 48130

We operate a distinctive and ethical publishing philosophy in all areas of our business, from our global network of authors to production and worldwide distribution.

Contents

Preface

Say not always what you know, but always know what you say.

Emperor Claudius, Tiberius Claudius Caesar
Augustus Germanicus (10 BCE – 54 CE)

With this preface I actually have a confession to make. I used to dislike the Romans, almost as much as the Victorians! I remember vividly being on a Roman themed primary school trip to Chester, a city which is often considered the most Roman city in Great Britain. As part of this school trip, we were made to play lions and Christians in the ruins of the amphitheatre. Of course, in hopes of self-preservation I chose to be a lion but I didn't really want to maul my classmates and even in primary school I must have already been on my way to becoming a vegan. To me the activity seemed frightening, violent and gory, and so the Romans, by association (as this was their favourite pastime) were also deemed frightening, violent and gory by seven-year-old me. Being Welsh also hasn't helped; our ancient Druids, my ancestors, didn't do so well in the Roman take over and perhaps I've not forgiven them yet! However, in this way, the Romans for me have been a lesson; offering a reminder that when we judge others solely for what we perceive as their mistakes, we fail to see the good in what and who we are judging.

Over the years since my amphitheatre experience, I have come to respect the Romans. They *were* into violent and gory entertainment and obsessed with rotten fish sauce but also brilliant and inspirational in their innovation, tenacity, organisation skills and ambition. They are well known for their mastery as lawyers, soldiers and engineers and I want to also personally thank them for toilets, hot baths and bound books! This book is also written in an alphabet that is owing to them and as I get travel sickness I am also pretty appreciate of straight roads!

It is also important to remember that the people of the past were humans just like us. Not characters in a dusty history book but humans with feelings, hopes, dreams, desires. Like you, every Roman Emperor, slave, priest and Roman citizen was wonderfully unique and had their fair share of bad habits, as well as skills, knowledge and virtues.

I was reminded of this during my short time volunteering in the amphitheatre archaeological dig at Chester (the same amphitheatre in which I was a lion ten years before!). While there I had the honour of holding ancient Roman poo, found minutes before within the cess pit beneath the amphitheatre's facilities. It was still perfectly intact and shaped, but surprisingly large! It might not sound like something to brag about but for me it was a momentous moment to which there should have been epic music playing in the background. I wondered – and still do – who did this come from? Maybe a gladiator, a spectator or someone selling their wares during the entertainment? Was he sat on the loo considering his next meal, regretting the last one or anxious about his forthcoming fight? Did the Romans read newspapers on the toilet, compose poetry or was he moaning about his wife to his mate? Who was he as a human-being, where did he come from, what were his hopes for the future? When we remember that the ancient Romans pooed, ate, breathed, laughed and cried maybe we can have allowance for their choices that we find less savoury and find compassion for the decisions and actions we now deem as wrong.

This book is about the religion of the ancient Romans, that intimate and personal belief system that was felt in the body and heart as hope, love, fear and pride, and stirred, awakened and fulfilled in the soul. It is the closest we can get to finding out what made the ancient Romans' tick; religion and spirituality is the doorway that opens us to the places deepest within ourselves and others. The religion of ancient Rome is also a belief system that was played out in the public sphere and found personal belief influenced and moulded by public opinion, laws, and traditions. In turn the public religion of ancient Rome was also dictated by politics and economy, as well as by the personal ambitions, requirements and desires of those with power and influence. With an empire so large and a history so full it will not be possible to personalise or individualise this brief introduction to ancient Roman religion but I hope as you read that you are reminded of the humans that lived and breathed it; from the solider that prayed to Mithras to survive one more battle, to the wife who diligently honoured Goddess Orbona in the hopes of finally having a child that survived its first years.

Perhaps from reading about the beliefs, hopes and practices of the ancient Romans you will also feel inspired or motivated to create your own spiritual practice, formed around the Roman deities or religious tools and traditions. As always with my books, this one is a mix of history and magic; what was and what can be. I offer you primary and archaeological sources along with modern interpretations but my priority is always to support your well-being and greatest healing and revelation of Self. The ancient Roman pantheon has certainly offered me many moments of revelation, integration and affirmation since my lion man-eating experience! How ever you chose to connect to the religion of ancient Rome I hope that you feel connected to the people that created it and can find some way to thank them for their legacy, from which we can now create our own empowered practice and choices. Ultimately, I hope in reading this book that you gain an insight into what was important for the ancient Romans, those very real people with the same basic needs and desires as your own. Perhaps like marmite you either love or dislike the Romans, but through this book you will begin to understand them regardless.

Timelines

Mythological Timeline of Rome

Chaos

Chaos births Janus

The Age of Janus (The Doorway)

The Age of Saturn (The Golden Spring)

The Age of Jupiter (Silver, Bronze, Iron)

Reign of Faunus in Latium, in which the hero Evander arrives and settles near the Tiber

Hercules visits Evander and defeats the Monster Cacus

Trojan occupation of the port city of Lavinium by Aeneas

Alban Dynasty of Latium

Lives of Romulus and Remus and the foundation of the city of Rome on Palatine Hill

The Rape of the Sabine Women

The reign of Numa

The suicide of Lucretia

The Republic

The Caesars and the Imperial Age

Timeline of Central Western Italy

All dates are approximate

c.1100 – c.900 BCE	Villanovan Culture (Developed into the Etruscan civilisation)
c.1000 – 338 BCE	Latin Civilisation (338 BCE Roman victory over the Latin States)
c.900 – 290 BCE	Sabine Civilisation (290 BCE Rome conquers the Sabines)
c.900 – c.200 BCE	Etruscan Civilisation (146 BCE Subjection to Rome)
509 BCE – 476 CE	Roman Civilisation

Significant Events in Rome

753 BCE	Traditional founding of Rome by Romulus
753 – 716 BCE	Latin Civilisation (338 BCE Roman victory over the Latin States)

Kings of Rome

753 BCE	Traditional founding of Rome by Romulus
753 – 716	BCE Reign of Romulus, the first King of Rome
715 – 672 BCE	Reign of Sabine King Numa Pompilius.
673 – 641 BCE	The Warrior King Tullus Hostilius, Rome's third king, expands the city's territory by conquering a neighbouring settlement. Rome's population is doubled.
600 BCE	The Latin language is first written in a script that is still used today.
510 BCE	The Temple of Capitoline is completed on Capitoline Hill, the first temple on this hill.
509 BCE	Tarquin, the last Etruscan king of Rome is expelled and the Republic is founded.

The Republic

500 BCE	Approx. date of the Capitoline Wolf bronze statue and the Apollo of Veii
451 BCE	Twelve Tables of Law published
396 BCE	Rome's destruction of the Etruscan town of Veii, heralding the following amalgamation of Etruria into Roman territory
390 BCE	The Gauls make a night attack on the city of Rome, yet it was saved by the raised alarm of the geese from the Temple of Juno
320 BCE	By this time the Legions of the Republic had been established
312 BCE	Construction of Rome's first aqueduct and the building of the first major Roman road, Via Appia
200's BCE	Rome's first prose writer Fabius Pictor writes a history of Rome
250 BCE	Rome controls most of Italy

204 BCE	Arrival of the Great Mother in Rome. The 'Black Stone' or Goddess Cybele brought to Rome from Anatolia
100 BCE	Temple of Neptune is built in Rome
90 – 89 BCE	Lex Julia: Grants of Roman Citizenship given to all Italians
46 BCE	Julian Calendar begins
44 BCE	Julius Caeser Assassinated
27 BCE	Augusts Crowned Emperor

The Empire

37 BCE	Building begins of the Temple of Mars Ultor in Augustus' Forum in Rome
30 BCE	Virgil begins writing the Aeneid.
17/18 CE	Death of the poet Ovid
50 CE	Rome is the largest city in the world – population around 1 million people
64 CE	Great Fire of Rome, in which the regions subura, palatine and the circus maximus were destroyed and the temple of Jupiter Optimus Maximus is set on fire
79 CE	Eruption of Mount Vesuvius and death of Pliny the Elder
80 CE	The colosseum first opens to the public and is dedicated with a festival and 100 days of games
109 CE	Tacitus publishes Histories
117 CE	Roman Empire reaches its greatest extent
118 – 28 CE	Building of the Pantheon in Rome by Emperor Hadrian
212 CE	Every free man in the empire is made a citizen by law
270's CE	Temple of the Sun built in Rome.
313 CE	Emperor Constatine issues Edict of Milan, which accepted Christianity. Ten years later it became the official religion of the Roman Empire.
324 – 30 CE	Constantinian foundation of Constantinople as New Rome

386 CE	Removal of Altar of Victory from Senate House; campaign against pagans begins
392 CE	Paganism banned by Theodosius I
476 CE	Last emperor Romulus Augustulus deposed by mercenary chief Odoacer

Introduction

Be present as I found the city, Jupiter and father Mars and mother Vesta, and take heed, all gods whom it is dutiful to summon. Under your auspices may this work of mine rise. Long may its life be, and the power of the ruling land, and let the rising and the setting day be subject to it.

Prayer for Rome by Romulus. Ovid, *Fasti*, Book 4

By the imperial age of ancient Roman history, the Empire had become so vast that the cultures, languages and religions that lived underneath its roof were incredibly diverse. Rather than trying to include the different religious features and aspects of the whole Roman Empire and all its peoples, this book will narrow right in, and pin point to the beating heart of that vast empire, to the city of Rome itself. It will cover the principal features and main characteristics of the Roman pantheon; that is, the gods and goddesses and religion of the ancient city of Rome. It will also explore how the people of that city practised that religion and worshipped their gods. There are boundaries and features that made the ancient Roman religion what it was and made it clearly defined within the large and diverse tapestry of the Empire and it is these features which I will consider throughout the following chapters.

In this book I share with you the ins and outs of not only the Roman pantheon and its principal deities but also what these deities meant for the people of Rome and *how* they connected to them and *why* they held them as important. Such an exploration involves not merely the deities themselves but also how the idea of them influenced the people of Rome in their daily and seasonal rituals. I will also consider the idea of legacy and tradition and how respect for the ancestors was deeply connected to Rome's gods and goddesses. This will involve considering what it meant to practice religion as a solider, mother, priestess or emperor, as well as how the very infrastructure of the city and landscape of Rome both influenced, and was influenced by, the religious beliefs, ideas and hopes of its people.

Who Were the Romans?

The Romans are those people of the Eternal City, that are known for enjoying central heating and luxurious bath houses, as well as reforming the calendar, building very long walls, giving the 'thumbs down' and shouting 'hail' at various Caesars while nibbling fried dormouse. They are also responsible for many of the laws, codes and traditions that form the basis of modern international law and politics today.

In this book when I refer to 'the Romans' I mean primarily those pertaining to the city of Rome and its surrounding districts, from the time period around the birth of Rome 753 BCE to roughly the end of the Severan dynasty (235 CE). This is the time frame from which the primary sources I explore pertain from.

The Greek historian, Timaeus of Tauromenium, was the first to date the foundation of Rome, and gave it as 814/813 BCE. Myths written down primarily in the 1st century BCE and 1st century CE, put forward the belief that the first beginnings of the city of Rome may have been at the same time as the Trojan War. In the 1st century BCE, a very exact date was decided by the Romans[1] and this was 21st April 753 BCE. This was the date when it was deemed the first King and demi-god, Romulus, founded the city himself. All of these foundation dates were attempts to organise and understand the concept and ideas of time and identity, and to give Rome its own mythology and origin story, in comparison and relation to other cultures and their timelines.

The first people of the city of Rome are believed to be migrants and settlers from the cultures and peoples around the area of western central Italy. They were a mix of Etruscan, Sabine and Latin people, that settled on and around the seven hills, next to the river Tiber. Archaeological evidence has remains of human presence on the site of the seven hills that dates the site as far back as 1500 BCE, the middle bronze age. Some speculate that this evidence is of the aboriginal people of the region, before other Italic cultures expanded into this area. By 1300 – 1100 BCE there is further archaeological evidence of occupation and burials in the marshy grounds beneath the hills. Around the 10th – 9th centuries BCE these seven hills and their associated huts became a small village, possibly villages, or perhaps even, as many argue, a pre-Roman settlement called *Septimontium* ('seven hills'). There are many rich graves found from this time which indicate a developing social structure.

There is then a period when this settlement grows and is ruled by chiefs or kings and is populated by peoples of Sabine, Latin and Etruscan origin. At this time the settlement becomes the pre-dominant one in the area. By the early sixth century the village has become a large town with temples, defensive walls and public buildings and a square that later becomes the Forum. In 509 BCE Rome becomes a republic. Eventually a large urban settlement or city called Rome developed that was forever the nucleus, even when Rome stretched far beyond its original boundaries. At this time the area surrounding Rome was primarily characterised by Etruscan beliefs, culture and dominance.

By 270 BCE, Rome had conquered most of what we now call Italy, including the Greek cities of the south, amalgamating the various areas to a whole body with Rome the beating heart. By the first century BCE Rome had more than a million inhabitants and the city was well on its way to becoming the central hub for the largest European empire in history. Rome's dominion over the known Mediterranean world by the first century CE, was viewed by the Romans as both inevitable and divinely ordained. By this time, a pillar of belief, supported by religious sentiment, had solidified in the Roman mind and heart, that this dominion was ultimately made possible by Roman *Virtus*; virtus being the qualities of a Roman, which were piety, fidelity, courage, strength and dignity. As we shall see this virtus was both inspired and affirmed by the deities and heroes of the Roman pantheon.

The earliest peoples of Rome were primarily farmers and those intimately connected to the land. Rome was made from a rich agricultural and pastoral heritage and this formed and influenced its religion and its religious structures and beliefs, even throughout its growth and expansion. Almost all the religious festivals, rituals and ceremonies had connections to farming, and seasonal changes and thresholds, as well as, the Roman's relationship with the land and its produce. The deities of the pantheon were all connected in some way to home and land and the practices of agriculture, fertility and protection; the three primary considerations of ancient people. The God Janus and Goddess Vesta were connected to the home, Saturn, Ops and Ceres to grain and grain production, Mars to protecting the fields and fertile growth. Jupiter was honoured and worshipped for the rain he would bring to the crops and land. Volcanus was the earthly fire, as well the natural phenomenon of earthquakes and volcanoes and he governed the production of agricultural implements.

You will find many different Roman deities mentioned in this book, some well-known such as Jupiter and Juno, and others less so, such as the Goddess Juturna, goddess of wells and springs and the God Quirinal, one of the most significant and important gods for the early Romans. However, I have given principal focus to the Di Selecti ('Chosen Ones') and explore them in most depth, as these are the deities that were considered the twenty principal deities of Rome. I will briefly mention many other deities in this book as it is important to remember that Rome was a city of many gods and cults, a place where even foreign deities, such as Isis, Mithras and Cybele, were sometimes officially welcomed and even grew huge followings. The vast pantheon outside of the Di Selecti broadened as the horizon of the Roman empire did. As a political policy, the Roman authorities tolerated the religions of the people they conquered. This religious tolerance and inclusivism of Rome led to it often being joked that Rome had more statues of deities and ancestors than living inhabitants. A joke that also hints at Rome's interest in religious art and devotional acts of service.

The Roman gods themselves also had diversity and adaptability in their nature and could be known by many names, depending on the function or theme they were serving or the concept they were portraying. One such example is Goddess Fortuna, who in some of her various manifestations is known as Fortunae Huiusce Diei (Fortune of the Present Day), Fortuna Primigenia (Fortune of the First-born), as well as Fortuna Conservatrix (Fortune as the Goddess of Fate and Luck). She is given a different epithet depending on function or the particular fortune her worshipper is hoping for. Each of these different aspects or forms of Fortuna also had their own temples and festivals. Fortuna Huiusce, for example, has her own temple in the sacred temple of Largo Argentina, dated to 101 BCE and there is also the temple of Fortuna Primigenia, just outside of Rome in Palestrina, where newborns were taken for blessings.

The same epithets could also be given to different deities. Fortuna's epithet conservatrix was also given to Juno, and even sometimes to Venus and Victory. The epithet would differ slightly depending on the god or goddess if was given to. Juno, as sovereign queen and goddess of marriage, could perhaps bestow good luck and a blessed fate in terms of marriage, domestic harmony and the good fortune of finding a spouse. Whereas Fortuna Conservatrix may bless you with a more generalised good luck. She could help you to get that promotion at work you wanted, or you may have wanted to make an offering of thanks to her for having chanced upon a lucky situation.

Sometimes deities also personified a virtue, such as in the case of victory as the Goddess Victoria and the Goddess Pietas, whom we will explore later in greater detail. There are also anthropomorphic deities who were non-human in form but given human roles or functions and sometimes personalities. Examples of these spirits of nature or divine elementals are the eternal flame vesta, the river god Tiber and she-wolf goddess Lupa. That these deities remain in the Roman pantheon well into the imperial age highlights to us the continued importance of the deities that Rome inherited from its very distant past, those deities that were of a time when God *was* nature, and nature *was* God, not merely a deity using it and choosing to manifest as it.

As for the evidence to guide us in understanding Roman religion, we do not have many accounts written by contemporaries in the very early centuries of Roman history (tenth to sixth centuries BCE). The evidence we do have is almost completely archaeological and funerary in nature. However, both of these do give a glimpse into the lives and beliefs of men, women, children, adults, slaves, warriors and kings. We do also have the reconstruction of, and commentary about, early Roman history, from later Romans (from fourth century BCE onwards) and also the works of Greek Historians who were keenly watching a growing state and warily observing its spread towards them. Some of these figures, both Greek and Roman, observe, criticise and celebrate their own Roman time, place and religion, as well as looking back to their forebears.

In the later Roman period, from the end of the republic onwards, we have much that has survived as written evidence. We can learn more about the Romans and their religious belief from poetry, satires, novels, histories, geographies, speeches, letters, essays, graffiti, wall paintings, talismans and jewellery, funerary memorials, writing tablets, shopping lists, account books, gravestones, biographies, coinage and even gladiator fan devotionals. There is also a useful amount of what we would call 'How to manuals' of a scientific, medical and engineering kind. These primary sources remind us of the everyday presence of the divine in Roman life. Sometimes deities are name dropped, such as in Catullus' poetic words *"The woman I love says that there is no one whom she would rather marry than me, not if Jupiter himself were to woo her"* (Poem 70). Other times we find deeply personal devotions expressed in tombstones such as that *'To the Divine Shades, from Aurelius Achilles, solider of the 8th praetorian cohort, made for his Valentinus, who lived five years and five months, a father for his sweetest son who well deserved it'*.[2] All of the above sources have formed the source material for this book and you will find many ancient Roman quotes throughout this book to enjoy!

From this diversity of sources this book does attempt to share what religion meant to almost *all* the people of Rome, from Caeser's personal preferences, to the rituals involved in the birth of children, so that you can have a rounded and broad viewpoint. This is a brief introduction of the practices of the priests and the farmers *and* the religious sensibilities of both mothers and soldiers. And so, we will explore the various forms of religious belief and practice from the small household observances to the grand public ceremonies of state.

It is worth noting, however, that this book is intended to be a place where history meets well-being, where archaeology meets spirituality. It is not just a history book; it is a place where you can learn more about the religion of ancient Rome and also consider a pathway to enriching your own spiritual practice. The invitation is that perhaps you may find some personal and spiritual fulfilment from learning about past belief systems and then find your own way of embodying, emulating or honouring them, if you feel you wish to. I value alternative sources such as the akashic records, energetic frequency and genetic and psychic memory, as well as historical ones, and these sources have contributed to the third part of this book.

Ultimately my aim in my work and writing is to support you in authentic and empowered living, to heal your wounds through embodied mythology, to grow in wisdom through historical insight, to remember your destiny in witnessing others living theirs and to find peace and fulfilment in your spiritual choices, whatever they may be.

It is my motto that knowledge is wasted unless transformed or transmuted into wisdom, through embodiment. Don't let history get dusty on the book shelves, take it, make it yours, see it with open eyes, hold it in your heart, learn from it and be inspired to live an empowered life that makes the world a better place for everyone.

Once you have discovered more about the religion of ancient Rome, I have included in the later chapters of this book some points of connection and ideas for bringing the Roman pantheon into your life and spiritual practice. So, if the Roman deities speak to you, or the practices and beliefs of the ancient Romans inspire you then there are some practical ideas and suggestions for making elements of this belief system yours.

Here is a buffet of ancient Roman spiritual beliefs. Have a taste of what is on offer, enjoy, savour, consider, reflect, discuss, go back for seconds of what feeds your heart and soul, then take your favourite bits home in a doggy bag.

So, let us enter Rome on the Appian Way and journey through temple, bathhouses and palaces in search for the Roman deities and those that worshipped them.

Part I

Chapter 1

History

*Rome has grown since its humble beginnings that it is
now overwhelmed by its own greatness.*

Titus Livius (59 BCE – 17 CE)

Many Roman deities and spiritual practices were inherited from
the Latium, Etruscan and Sabine cultures that made up the first
peoples of the area of Rome[3]. The Romans could trace their
background and lineage, both of blood, culture and religion, to
all three of these peoples. Tradition has it that the first peoples
were a mix but some sources argue for each of Rome's hills being
home to a different and specific tribal village of immigrants,
settlers or aborigines of the area. In mythology, the founder of
Rome, Romulus set up his settlement on Palatine Hill and his
brother Remus on the Aventine. They brought with them the
Latin people from their homeland of Latium, south of Rome and
the outcasts, supporters and entrepreneurial from the Etruria
lands; the lands in which they were raised. Contemporary
Roman writers and historians argue that after Romulus it is also
possible that Etruscans from the North of Rome populated the
Caelian or Viminal Hills. There is archaeological evidence to
support the folklore that the Sabines, who were to the east of
Rome, arrived in Rome after the Latins. Evidence is found for
the Sabine's settling and living in villages on the Quirinal and
Esquiline hills. Interestingly these Sabine people also share a
Wolf centred origin story, similar to that of Rome's Romulus
and Remus. Specific deities and triads were originally, and
then continued to be, linked with each hill and village, such as
Goddess Ceres and the Aventine Hill.

All three peoples had their own distinct languages and traditions; however, it is believed that eventually they all came together for purposes of common worship. In his history of Rome, written in the 1st century, Plutarch shares a beautifully poetic moment when the different peoples of this area all came together under Romulus's leadership:

And so, a circular trench was dug around what is now Comitium and in it they deposited the first fruits of all things that are essential to life or deemed precious by custom. Finally, each man brought a small portion of earth from his native land and threw it in among the fruits, so that everything was now mixed together. The Romans call this trench by the same word they use to describe the heavens, which is mundus. With this as its centre, the Romans then laid out their city around it in a circle.

Plutarch, *The Rise of Rome, Romulus, 11*

In this ceremony we also get a glimpse of the beginnings of later Roman religious practices of designation, dedication and preparation of sacred land for temples building. The defining of boundaries was important for an area that was populated by several different tribes. However, even when the people of Rome later established their own new identity as Romans, the same original practices remained pillars of the institution of Roman religion.

As the first peoples of the area of Rome, it is from the Etruscans, Sabine and Latins that Roman religion inherited the majority of its deities, religious practices and ideas of the afterlife. Of the three it was the Etruscan culture that was Rome's greatest influence on religion, architecture, culture and art. The traditional founding date of Rome, 753 BCE approximately marks the time when the influence of Etruria influence began on this small area of Italy on the edge of the Tiber. The Etruscans certainly were the most powerful and richest peoples in the area during the time of Rome's growth from village to city and controlled much of central and northern Italy from the 9th century BCE until the rise of an independent city of Rome. First the Villanovans and then their descendants the Etruscans were the people of the area that the Romans called Etruria, which is roughly now modern-day Tuscany and northern Lazio, mid-west Italy. Many of the sacred sites where Etruscans worshipped were Villanovan first and both tended to open air sanctuaries with temples made of wood or sun-dried brick, as stone was kept for the dead. It is for this reason that the majority of archaeological finds for these peoples are funerary in nature.

Upon the walls of the Etruscan tombs, we find the origins of gladiatorial combat in funeral games and duels. In Etruria the *munera* (obligations or duties) performance of a fight between two 'gladiators' would often follow the death of a chieftain, and was an important part of the ritual celebrations of his life. In an imitation of this earlier practice the earliest gladiatorial fight to have been held in the city of Rome was recorded to have been in 264 BCE during a nobleman's funeral. However, by the time of the Colosseum, the original ritual and religious aspect of gladiatorial fights seems to have been lost and they became mere entertainment. Circus games, boxing matches and possibly chariot racing were also of Etruscan origin. The Romans also continued the Etruscan practice of burying the dead on the sides of roads going out of the towns and cities. Early Roman statues of deities were often made of terracotta and sometimes gilded with bronze and early Etruscan bronze statues boast some astonishing works of highly skilled and executed religious art. Plutarch in *The Rise of Rome* shares that by tradition, Romulus, following the death of his brother,

*...turned to the foundation of his city. He first summoned men
from Etruria, who guided and instructed him in every detail,
so that everything was done in strict accordance with sacred
rites and formulas, as if in a religious ceremony*
Plutarch, *The Rise of Rome, Romulus, 11*

From the Etruscans the Romans translated the *Disciplina Etrusca*,
volumes upon volumes of religious lore and these may have
served as a backbone to some religious practices. The *Disciplina
Etrusca* included the *Book of Entrails*, which offered interpretation
of the liver of a sacrificed animal; the *Book of Thunderbolts*, which
supported the interpretation of thunder and lightning, of which
they were many variations, all related to, or the manifestation
of, nine different gods, and the *Book of Rituals*, which was a
guide to founding cities and temples in collaboration with the
divine. Two important practices that we know for certain were
inherited from Etruscans and prolifically used by the Romans
was hepatoscopy and augury, both prophetic divining of the
future by observation of bird and animal behaviour and their
entrails.

As for deities, many of the well-known deities of the city
of Julius Ceaser can find a root in the religion of these early
settlers of Rome. The earlier tribes of the areas surrounding
Rome believed that all growing things were inhabited by forces,
spirits or beings that needed to be placated if things were to
go well and the life of the community assured. The Etruscan
Gods and goddesses were intrinsically connected to nature and
natural phenomenon. To the Etruscans all held spirit and all
was sacred and the gods communicated through signs in nature
and manifested through natural occurrences. Deities such as
Venus and Mars began as spirits of fertility, vegetation, land
and plants and Juno and Jupiter as elementals of the air and
sky. Most of the names for the Etruscan deities were gender
neutral and did not have the anthropomorphic qualities of the

later Roman gods. The God that we now know as Jupiter, for the Etruscans was called Tinia (also Tin, Tinh, Tins or Tina) who was the deity of rain, sky and storms. There was also the Roman goddess, Minerva, who was originally known as Menvra, Menrfa or Menarva, and she was Etruscan deity of craft, art, medicine and wisdom. Venus can be found as Turan, spirit of fertility, vegetation, vitality and birds, and was patroness of the city of Velch. The Roman God, Neptune, was known as the deity Nethuns, Etruscan God of wells and spring water.

The Goddess, Juno Curitis, has her origins with the Sabine people, yet Juno by other names was also worshipped by the Latins and the Etruscans. In Etruria she was the deity, Uni, or Uno, who was the supreme deity of the Etruscan city of Veii and she was a goddess of the sky. Other deities seem to have their origins in ancient Latium, such as Diana whose ancient shrine was at the location of the settlement of Alba Longa, the ancestral seat of Romulus and Remus and the Latium kings. Vulcan as Vulcanus also had Latin origins, as did Vesta, whose Vestal Virgins are one of the oldest Italian sects of female priestesses. The temples of Vesta and Vulcan are also two of the oldest sites in ancient Rome and both connected to very ancient fire cults. There always remained an awareness of the gods as, of, and connected to nature, whether nature was a manifestation of the gods, used by them or home to them. Throughout the history of ancient Rome, religion was an essential aspect of Roman life and nearly every activity and aspect of life was connected to the divine, whether that be a deity, ancestor, elemental or a spirit.

The first rulers of the Rome, the Latin, Sabine and Etruscan kings of the 8th – 6th century BCE, were also credited by later Romans with the invention or introduction of many of its religious institutions. By tradition Romulus, grandson of a Latin king and the first of Rome, in the 8th century BCE built the first temple of Jupiter in Rome, as well as the temples of Vulcan and Vesta, and initiated many of the rites and rituals associated with his father, Mars. His successor, Numa Pompilius, a Sabine King of Rome, was credited with much of what we now know as ancient Roman religious structure and even with creating the title and role Pontifex or head priest for his priesthood. Numa was celebrated for his piety and it was said that much of what he shared and introduced was knowledge given to him by his Goddess lover and through regular communion with deities. The construction of the temple of Jupiter on Capitoline Hill was by tradition undertaken by the two kings Tarquinius Priscus and Tarquinius Superbus. The creation day of all these shrines and temples were known as the foundation dates and were marked on the religious calendars. These foundation days of temples became holy or birth days of the associated deity. Festivals recreated and celebrated the original dates and continued to do so well into the imperial age over half a century later.

So, Rome grew up as a branch from earlier Italian civilisations, yet it eventually sought and gained its independence and became not only a separate culture and people, but rival, enemy, ruler. By the 5th century BCE and the time of the republic 'to be Roman' was a concept and the city of Rome had an identity separate to those earlier roots, even if they were never forgotten. Later Roman Historians and writers from the republic onward even went so far as to judge the Etruscans to be somewhat wild and pleasure seeking and remembered with some measure of horror how Etruscan men and women openly showed public affection and got drunk and danced together!

By the time we get to the 1st century CE, Rome would have looked back on its foundations and the first Roman people much as we do to the early medieval people, with Romulus very much the Roman equivalent of King Arthur. It is a large stretch of time in which much developed and changed in terms of politics, architecture and economy. However, many ancient Roman religious ideas and concepts remained a constant thread through all of this time. Religion even sometimes offers a point of continuity in a rapidly expanding and changing world. In the 1st century CE, for example, there was an increase of writing, commentary, epics and annals (many of which created or documented mythology for the first time) which show us that Roman citizens were still holding tight to beliefs, rituals and practices of many hundreds of years in the past. So, let us next explore the sacred knowledge and mythology that the Roman's held so dear and discover the stories of the first citizens such as Romulus and Numa and how mythology, cosmology and philosophy had a central role in shaping the religion of ancient Rome.

Chapter 2

Sacred Knowledge

The presence of the gods gives the past a certain dignity,
and if any nation deserves to be allowed to claim that its
ancestors were gods, that people is our own.
Livy, in the preface of *History*

In this chapter will we explore what I call sacred knowledge. Sacred knowledge is the knowledge that was given divine or sacred status and importance by the ancient Romans, and contributed to, or influenced, their religious practices, superstitions and spiritual beliefs. This sacred knowledge includes the foundation stories and mythology of Rome, as well as cosmology, astrology and philosophy. Many of Rome's recorded histories were described or considered 'Annals' and I believe this in itself hints that the history of Rome and her people *was* deemed sacred. Choosing to call one's work 'Annals', meaning priestly records, is a choice by writers such as Tacitus, Fabius and Ennius and compares their 'historical' works to the official annual records of Roman priests, such as lists of religious events. Calling the compilations of historical and mythological records 'Annal' gave them a religious or sacred authority or validation.

So, the exploration and recording of history, mythology and the workings of the universe was considered sacred by the ancient Romans but why were epics and treatise written, was it just about written a record of the divine? And how much of their content was common knowledge? Myths and legends, as well as philosophy, astrology and cosmology are recorded extensively by writers such as Livy and Virgil but also mentioned in passing by significant figures of the Roman world such as Cicero and Pliny. Some myths, legends, annals and treatise were written for political reasons and with political funding, objectives and others sought out the traditional and oral history of the time, or shared that which was known as public opinion. Other writers recorded history and mythology for poetic, literary and philosophical purposes, such as Ovid in *Metamorphosis, the* collection of Graeco-Roman myths and legends. Virgil wrote the story of the hero Aeneas as much for the expression of his skill as a writer, as he did for celebrating Emperor Augustus. Historians now believe that many of these important works, such as Virgil's *Aeneid,* were created to be spoken aloud and performed for small audiences rather than large theatrical productions or commercial books, while other texts were intended solely for prosperity and others were personal pieces of writings, such as letters, poems and dairies. By the time of the late republic and empire epics and mythology had also become part of Roman education, that is, the education available to primarily the children of Roman noblemen. There have been fragments of the *Aeneid* found as far away as Hadrian's Wall, which tells us that there must have been some knowledge of classical tales and philosophical ideas spread via literature even throughout the empire.

For the masses of Rome, mythological stories were shared in pantomime and mine, both of which became popular in the 1st century BCE. Aspects of foundation stories, myths and legends also found their way into plays at the theatre, as well as the symbology, art and ritual of religious festival, practices and temples, and in coinage, mosaics and statues. Therefore, we could consider the sacred knowledge I am about to share with you, as general knowledge. Stories first and foremost owe their survival to oral transmission. Consider how often we still tell and use the stories of Robin hood or King Arthur now. We can perhaps assume the foundation stories of Rome and their deities would have had the same hold over popular mind and may have been as well-known as current affairs.

Aspects of myth, legend, philosophy, cosmology and astrology all had social significance and had an effect on human behaviour, from the timetabling of daily regimes, the decoration of favourite legends on the dining room wall, to the totem one chose to have around one's neck. The inclusion of the names, symbols and worship of the deities in story, poems, song and art would have made them very real and very present. The great epic writers Virgil and Livy used their writing skills to put into poetic written word that which was already known, loved, feared and believed. Through exploring epics, myths and philosophies we are therefore given a glimpse into the dreams, ideas, reflections, hopes and principles of the ancient Roman people.

Foundation Stories

If men could choose their own birthright, no one would be poor and no one would be of low station; each and every man would find a happy home. But given that such decisions are out of our hands, we must submit to the natural order of things, and accept whatever fortune is appointed us. And so, we must be judged by what we make of ourselves.
Seneca the Elder (1st century BCE – 1st century CE)

In this chapter the mythologies that I choose to highlight in particular are the foundation stories of Rome. A story tells you not just about the hero and the characters but also something about the storyteller/author and the reader/listener. The foundation stories of Rome form and reflect the very basis of ancient Roman ideas of belonging and identity. These foundation stories tell us 'What did it mean to be Roman?', by showing us the values that were so important that they were personified by great heroes. And why did certain gods interfere in Rome's rise and how did that affirm the belief in Rome's destiny?

We have been left with two distinct foundation stories for ancient Rome. The first, that of Romulus and Remus, is Italian and deeply rooted in ancient Latin, Etruscan and Sabine traditions, practices and beliefs. It is a compilation of oral histories, beliefs and traditions shared and passed down from the early days of the settlement of Rome that celebrate the ancestry of the Roman people. It is a story that demonstrates how divine favour and determination can support one in triumph over adversity and humble beginnings.

The second, written down in an epic poem by Virgil in the 1st century BCE, is that of the hero Aeneas and is Roman and Greek in its influence. It borrows grandeur associated with a great city of the past, Troy, and seeks to emulate the hero story. It gives Rome one of its own heroes and epics in the vein of Greek poetic tradition, because after all, an illustrious city requires an illustrious founder. The *Aeneid* also features and makes reference to the other (but no lesser) hero of Roman mythology, Evander, son of the Goddess Carmenta. He was believed to be the first human ruler of the area around what came to be Rome. All these stories were also shared in part by the writers Horace, Ovid, Plutarch and Dionysius of Halicarnassus.

There was a Roman tendency to accept their mythology as part of history, that anything was truly possible. This belief and trust in the potentiality of the divine and humans was perhaps the same energy that enabled the idea of an empire to succeed. As we shall see, ancient Roman myth and legend, or perhaps more so the decision to write it down and record it, played its most important role in the affirmation of Roman ancestry – what it meant to be Roman and what made Romans different to others – and, ultimately affirmed legacy and pietas as important contributions to the greatness of Rome and her people.

The Aeneid

These shall be your skills: to impose peace, spare the conquered and overthrow the mighty.
Virgil, *Aeneid*, Book 6

The *Aeneid* is an epic poem, that shares the events that led up to founding of Latium. It was written by Virgil and commissioned by Emperor Augustus. It was in part commissioned to subtly affirm the authority and divinity of the Julian family (Gaius *Julius* Caeser) that claimed their descent from Aeneas, but also for the glory and celebration of the mighty Roman state and its people. It was written when ancient Rome and its people were well established, when the earliest history of Rome was already mythology. There were many stories and oral histories about the foundation of Rome and its ancestors but Virgil as a master storyteller pulled together many threads, added a few of his own from his scholarly background and created a tapestry of his own making in written poetic form. He was also influenced by Homer in his writing and was tasked with the creation of an epic that could stand up without shame next to the *Iliad*. However, what makes the *Aeneid* different from the *Iliad* is the claims of trojan descent for the Romans, setting them apart, or reaffirming an opposition, to the Greeks. Virgil's work is significant because it influenced late Roman thought and hints at how in his time it was believed that Rome was actualising or fulfilling a prophetic legacy begun by the great heroes of the past. It has been argued that Augustus himself hoped this epic would prove inspiring and motivating and affirm the idea of a Rome destined for a greatness that was divinely ordained. However, Virgil asked in his will for it to be destroyed as he was worried about its misuse and to a certain extent regretted its creation. He died in 19 BCE and his wishes were not carried out.

For us it is an invaluable resource as it provides us with some insight into what was important for the ancient Romans; the desire to have their own epic tales and heroes such as the Greeks did, and maybe a wish to emphasise the importance of divinely orchestrated foundation of their city and empire. Personally, for Augustus, the documenting of such a history and reference to his lineage also offered validation for his reign and him personally and the epic highlights the role of the deities in being able to offer this validation through association and their patronage. Previously Julius Caeser had claimed lineage directly from Goddess Venus, via Aeneas in order to validate his dictatorship. The *Aeneid* is full of flattery and affirmation of the Julian family, with a motivation to validate their rule and affirm their divine ancestors.

The *Aeneid* is also invaluable as it provides us with insight into the Roman perspective during the 1st century BCE around themes such as 'what is hero', 'what are Rome's responsibilities as ruler?', as well as what is the price of victory, how were the gods viewed and how do they involve themselves in the lives of humans? The story centres around one man, but we are given glimpses of the grief and hopes of women, mothers and lovers, the practices of doctors, the regrets of old men and the aspirations of the young. It even offers us insights into the ideas of the underworld and the importance of piety, as epitomised and embodied by Aeneas and portrayed in his sacrifice to the penates, the household gods. Aeneas himself was a powerful example for the ancient Roman with regards to *pietas*. In the idea of him; through his dignity, honour and loyalty, he taught how to embody pietas, that is how to serve the gods, and one's family and city. He was a considered prime example of what it meant to be a Roman and how to serve the gods, your country and fellow man, dutifully, loyally and with complete devotion, above all else. Aeneas himself laments to the dead Dido

It was the stern authority of the commands of the gods that
drove me on.
Virgil, *Aeneid Book 6* (Lines 461 – 462)

Romulus and Remus

In my opinion it was pre-ordained that this great city should
be founded, and this mightiest of empires, second in dominion
only to the gods, should come into being.
Livy, *Histories Vol.1*

The legend of Romulus and Remus is arguably the most important story of Rome, as it is the foundation story of the city itself and emphasises the direct involvement of the divine in the creation and growth of Rome. The story was referenced by many ancient Romans, from politicians such as Cicero and Julius Ceaser, to historians, poets and philosophers such as Sallust, Ovid, Virgil and Plutarch. The fullest and most detailed accounts were written over seven hundred years after the events, from the 1st century BCE onwards, by the historians Livy and Plutarch and the poet Ovid, to whom we can credit with much of what we know of the story of Romulus and Remus today. However, before them the story seems to have been already very well-known and passed down via oral history, and in art, social traditions and ritual, long before it was first written down. There were many holy days, rites and rituals such as the Lupercalia and the Quirinalia, two of Rome's oldest festivals, that involved the re-telling and re-enactments of the story's significant events. Statues, iconography and religious items that pre-date the first literary accounts also depict the primary figures and players of the myth.

This story is rooted deeply in the geography of Rome, featuring the Tiber and Palatine Hill, places that you can still locate and visit today. A myth always feels personal and yours when you can walk its landscapes and interact with the deities involved, in the place they actually roamed. For the ancient Romans the foundation myth was located where they lived, slept, married and died. They walked daily upon the sacred land and could easily still visit the places that were central to life for their ancestors.

Romulus's story features many deities of Roman religion, such as the Goddess Luperca, the Gods Mars and Faustulus, and Father Tiber. Romulus and Remus were by birth demi-gods, though Romulus was later fully deified as the God Quirinius. Plutarch equated Romulus's status and deeds with that of the Greek hero Theseus, whom legend gave the credit of the political unification of the territory of Athens. The stories also include the vestal virgins, in the figure of Rhea Silvia, the Vestal mother of Romulus and Remus. Their inclusion and reference in the story remind us that their fire cult pre-dates to before the foundation of Rome. It is often hinted that their sacred fire perhaps could have been brought to Rome, to become its eternal flame, in honour of, or even by Rhea Silvia herself.

This story remained burning in the hearts of Ancient Romans as they marked with a sacred black stone the place of Romulus's hut and grave, created a temple in the cave of Lupa and build some of the most significant temples and imperial palaces upon the sacred hill of Palatine, continuing the tradition of royal residency right upon that holy hill. The fertility festival of Lupercalia also remembered both Goddess Luperca, her breastfeeding the twins and the circular run of Romulus that marked his cities boundaries. The traditional founding date of Rome by Romulus, 21st April 753 BCE was also marked and celebrated every April (though this date was calculated by later Roman historians to be a century or two too late). For many ancient Romans this story was not myth or legend but a true story, a history of their people and land and a history in which the divine was not just present but intimately involved. Statues of Romulus and Remus, and their milk nurse She-Wolf could be found all over ancient Rome, from the Forum, to Capitoline Hill. The belief in the truth of the foundation story was and is unquestionably important in understanding ancient Rome, the empire and its people.

In the story of Romulus and Remus, we begin in ancient Alba Longa. The King of Alba Longa, Numitor, is usurped by his brother Amulius. Numitor's daughter is imprisoned so she cannot bare an heir, but the God Mars impregnates her and she gives birth to Romulus and Remus. As babes their lives were turned upside down when their great Uncle Amulius, orders their death by drowning, so that he could eradicate those that posed a threat to his rule. He ordered them thrown in the River Tiber, however, instead they were placed in a basket that was carried by the high flood down the river to land at the paws of a waiting she-wolf on the banks of the Tiber at the base of Palatine Hill (in some other accounts the basket is never placed in the river but left on the bank and the she-wolf finds it there). The She-Wolf, Lupa, suckled the babes under a fig tree and fiercely defends them when attackers arrive. In some recounting she took them to her cave on Palatine Hill, they remained in safety there with her, the Lupercal, until they were taken by a shepherd Faustinus (later deified as Faustulus), who then raised them until they were old enough to seek revenge. Eventually they were reunited with their grandfather and the twins now men, together killed their great uncle and restored their grandfather Numitor to the throne of Alba Longa. They then go on to found their own settlements, Romulus upon the hill which they had been raised, Palatine, above the Lupercal cave and Remus upon the Aventine Hill. They argued over which location was the best site for a new foundation and eventually a deadly quarrel occurred when

Remus crossed a boundary line that Romulus had made with his plough. Augury was used to resolve their dispute over who should rule and where.

> *Then, with surprising care, for each desired to reign,*
> *They sought for omens from the birds.*
> *Remus, aloof, engrossed, scanned heaven for,*
> *A bird of favour. Handsome Romulus*
> *Sought his winged quarry high on Aventine.*
> *Should Rome or Remora be the city's name?*
> *And which should rule? The question filled their hearts.*
> Ennius, *Annals*. 33

The gods seemed to favour Romulus with their signs, and a fight ensued in which Romulus, or his men, killed his brother.

> *So, perish anyone who leaps over my walls.*
> Romulus slays his brother, Remus, in Livy's *History of Rome Vol.1*

Remus was traditionally believed to have been buried on the Aventine Hill, which still contained his sanctified grove in the 1st century BCE. It is Palatine Hill, where Romulus established the beginning of his town and it is an interesting side note that at the beginning of the 20th century archaeologists did in fact find the remains of Iron age huts on the Palatine Hill with a cave nearby deemed the fabled lair of the she-wolf. Romulus then populated the town by inviting outlaws and immigrants from the surrounding areas to join him and his warriors. Romulus was considered the first of the Kings of Rome, kings that reigned over these people until the founding of the Republic around 509 BCE.

Romulus the leader, warrior, hero and finally God, was deemed only to be matched in greatness by his successor, the pious and peace-bringing King Numa, who, as we shall see, was credited with the creation or introduction of the majority of ancient Roman religion.

Cosmology and Astronomy

Dwell on the beauty of life. Watch the stars, and see yourself running with them. Think constantly on the changes of the elements into each other, for such thoughts wash away the dust of earthly life.
Emperor Marcus Aurelius, *Meditations*

Cosmology

Cosmology examines the origin and evolution of the universe, and was a topic that was discussed in the ancient Roman world. Cicero writes in 45 CE, in *Scipio's Dream*, a poetic reflection on current cosmological ideas and both the poets Virgil and Ovid gave their own poetic versions of the beginnings of the universe. Marcus Manilius, a 1st century CE Roman astrologer and poet also wrote didactic poems on astrology and astronomy and shares an idea of Rome's power being part of the natural order of things. His *Astronomica* is the earliest Roman treatise on astrology and cosmology that we possess. In the introduction to his work, he credits the God Mercury as:

...the founder of this great and holy science; through you has man gained a deeper knowledge of the sky... that mankind might learn wherein lay God's greatest power
Book 1, Lines 25 and 37

And he honours astrological and cosmic knowledge as the gifts of Mercury, as well as honouring Apollo for being muse and tuner of the poem.

When it comes to the idea and theories of creation, Ovid writes of a universe that comes from chaos, chaos being a bland and empty concept before the vividness of life and existence. He shares that at the beginning,

Before the earth and the sea and the all-encompassing heaven came into being, the whole of nature displayed but a single face, which men have called Chaos; a crude, unstructured mass, nothing but weight without motion, a general conglomeration of matter composed of disparate, incompatible elements.
Ovid, *Metamorphoses, Book 1, Lines 59*

His work of myths and legends is centred around the theme of change, metamorphosis, and he depicts creation as fluid in its form, changeable, with the possibility of moving between the areas of earth, heavens, underworld and *all* things arriving and passing and each age like waves upon the shore. Ovid describes the creator as *"the god who is nature"* (Book 1.21) and puts forward the idea of a nameless being who creates and who is creation. God and nature are synonymous, a viewpoint also held by stoicism, the philosophy so highly regarded by the Emperor Marcus Aurelius. Ovid's creator from the chaos *'disentangled the elements'*, separating, ordering and departmentalising everything to its place. Some Romans held the belief that it was the God Janus who personified the original chaos and was the beginning and end of all things.

The poet Virgil shares the belief that Roman civilisation was a peak in a tapestry of creation that has had all its parts woven on purpose and put in their destined place. Virgil's beginning of the creation is shared in the Aeneid as:

In the beginning Spirit fed all things from within, the sky and the earth, the level waters, the shining globe of the moon and

the Titan's star, the sun. It was Mind that set all this matter in motion. Infused through all the limbs, it mingled with that great body, and from the union there sprang the families of men and animals, the living things of the air and the strange creatures born beneath the marble surface of the sea. The living force within them is of fire and its seeds have their source in heaven.

Virgil, *Aeneid, Book 6, Lines 724 -731*

The ancient Romans also knew, as it is written in many accounts, that the earth was a sphere, that the central part of the earth was hot and uninhabitable and that a temperate land covered the earth, an area which sat between two polar areas of cold and snow. It was also believed that humans were:

...moulded into the likeness of gods who govern the universe.

Ovid, Metamorphoses, 1.83

In general, it is believed that the ancient Romans took a view of creation and the universe that was inherited from the Latin and Etruscan people before them. There was a firm belief in a golden age that came before the time that was known and which had been overseen by benevolent gods. This age was ruled by Saturn, the Lord of Time. It was a perpetual spring when all was fertile and peaceful. This time, the time before Jupiter's birth, was also a time when there was no moon.[4]

Astronomy

Astronomy is the study of the form and content of the universe. The writer Ptolemy, writing in the middle of the 2nd century CE, created a compilation of seven centuries of accumulated knowledge and gives us great insight into what knowledge of the universe was available to the ancient Romans. In *Grand Compilation*, he also added his own observations and speculations that share perhaps an ancient Roman viewpoint on what was deemed possible, as well as his beliefs in the connection between the universe, music, harmony and the soul.

The Roman lawyer, Pliny the Elder, in his 1ˢᵗ century CE *Historia Naturalis* of thirty-seven volumes, also shares on a vast number of subjects including astronomy, meteorology and geography, those things, he states, that are not a product of man's manufacture. His viewpoint of the cosmos and world is argued to be that of a stoic but one that had a devoted and disciplined interest and thirst for knowledge of all things scientific.

In Book 2 of his *Natural Histories,* for example, he shares that thunderbolts come from three planets

> *...when they fall to the earth are termed thunderbolts are the fires of the three upper planets, particularly those of Jupiter, which is in the middle position – possibly because it voids in this way the chare of excessive moisture from the upper circle (of Saturn) and of excessive heart from the circle below (of Mars); and that is the origin of the myth that thunderbolts are the javelins hurled by Jupiter. Consequently, heavenly fire is spit from a burning log, bringing prophecies with it, as even the part of himself that he discards does not cease to function in its divine tasks.*
> Book 2.18

I also particularly like his description of the colours of the planets:

> *It is true that each has its own special hue – Saturn white, Jupiter transparent, Mars fiery, Lucifer bright white, Vesper glaring, Mercury radiant, the moon soft, the sun when rising glowing.*
> Book 2.16

Piny was not a scientist but states that his histories are in fact the recording of matters of importance. Like Pliny, the ancient Romans knew of the sun, the moon and the five planets that can be seen with the naked eye; Mercury, Venus, Mars, Jupiter and Saturn and these planets were associated with their corresponding deities. The sun and the moon were considered by most to be two of the seven planets, those celestial bodies that did move in an ocean of stars that were fixed in place (planet itself a word meaning *'wanderer'*).

Following the progress of the sun and moon in particular was practiced by the state to mark the calendar year and to regulate and structure periods of days and months. However, following the progress of the moon was also important for more personal reasons. Pliny the Elder advises that:

...it is thought, too, to be a preventative of baldness and of head-ache, to cut the hair on the seventeenth and twenty-ninth days of the moon.
Book 28, Chapter 5, lines 61-62

The idea of the universe that was the accepted at the time has the earth stationary at the centre of the universe, with the planets and stars circling around it.

...earth rests in the centre... The sun's heat and size can hardly be much greater or less than is perceived by our sense... The moon too, whether it shines with borrowed light illumining the world, or whether it sends its own light from its own body, whichever it is, its size, as it moves through the heavens, is no larger than it appears to our eyes as we see it...
Lucretius 152-153 *On the Nature of Things*

The earth was considered the *"hearth of the universe"* with the idea of a central fire at the centre of the earth that was likewise the centre of the universe.

Ovid when talking about the Temple of Vesta shares that,

*The shape of the temple is said to have been before what it now
remains, and plausible reason is to found for the shape. Vesta is
the same as the earth: an unsleeping fire is to be found in each.
Earth and the hearth signify their own place.*

*Earth, like a ball, resting on no prop, hangs with air beneath
it, so heavy a weight. Rotation itself keeps the glob balanced,
and there is no angle at all to press on the parts of it. And since
it is positioned at the centre of everything, so that it touches
no side more, or less, if it were not convex it would be closer to
one part, and the universe would not have Earth as its central
weight.*

Ovid, June 9th, *Fasti*

Also, important here is the use of the term Vesta as a synonym.
They also viewed the star systems anthropomorphically,
believing that the star patterns were gods, heroes, sacred
animals that had their own power and symbology. Many
heroes and heroines were immortalised as star constellations
and:

*…there are reasons why conceptions of the Gods are imprinted
on human minds … the fourth advanced, and the greatest, is
the uniform movement and undeviating rotation of the heavens,
the individuality, usefulness, beauty of order of the sun, moon
and stars, the very sight of which is sufficient proof that they
are not the outcome of chance.*

Cicero 52 *The Nature of the Gods*

Astrology

Astrology studies the effect of the planets, galaxies and stars on
the events and peoples of the earth or as Manilius puts it:

...the stars, by which the operation of divine reason diversify the chequered fortunes of mankind.
Astronomica, Book 1, Line 3,

Plutarch notes in *The Rise of Rome* that it was reported that on the founding day of Rome a sun and moon conjunction occurred and that the eclipse was deemed to be prophetic and offered its own sanctification of that day and its events. Romulus himself was said to have been born under a similarly significant total eclipse of the sun, the date and time calculated by the mathematician, Tarutius. By tradition he also ascended to heaven and became a God during a solar eclipse on the 7th July. Both astrological events were deemed to validate the sanctity of both the destiny of Rome and Romulus and affirm their divinity.

Astrologers were sought out by the ancient Romans, even by the emperors themselves. Tacitus writes that Emperor

Tiberius asked the astrologer Thrasyllus if he had read his own horoscope for the present year and day. Thrasyllus made calculations based on the position of the stars and their relation to each other. He hesitated, then showed fear. The closer he looked, the greater his astonishment and terror. He cried that he was facing a crisis which might prove fatal. Tiberius clasped him warmly, congratulated him on anticipating his danger and assuring him that he would escape it."
Annals 6, 21

Augustus and Agrippa were also noted to have consulted astrologers and were predicted fantastic futures, but the emperor Domitian had his astrologer Ascletario put to death when he was told his corpse would be ripped apart by dogs. It was illegal for anyone other than the emperor to consult an astrologer about an Emperor's future. Astrology was taken seriously by the Etruscans and Romans and sometimes was complimented by other forms of divination, such as haruspicy. However, astrologists sometimes suffered from repression and were frequently expelled from Rome.

As already discussed in cosmology, the Romans were interested in science and had an awareness of the stars, tracking and working with them for practical reason, that could also have mystical applications. Writers often share the position of constellations and stars and their place in the sky as well as their more symbolic significances. For example, Manilius shares about the twelve houses (or temples) of the night sky and their corresponding meanings for humankind, both of which are still used in astrology today. About the constellation of the charioteer, he says:

Next, bearing his footsteps near the crouching Bull comes the Charioteer whose calling won him heaven and a name … Jupiter hallowed it, as was its due, with a place among the eternal stars, repaying heaven gained with the gift of heaven.
Manilius, *Astronomica*, lines 361 and 369

Ovid also writes of the constellations, such as the northern plough and the zodiac signs of the charging bull, the centaur archer, the raging lion, the scorpion and crab, as well as how:

the signs which the brother travels through in a long year, the sister's horse pass through in one month.[5]
Fasti, Book 3, line 110

He also shares how the stars were used as heralds to important dates and the seasons:

[13 May] *You'll see all the Pleiades and the whole line of the sisters when there's one night left before the Idea. That ... is when summer begins and the times of the mild spring come to an end.*

Fasti, Book 5, Lines 599 – 602

Artists used personification of the phases of the day, as well as depicting zodiac signs, and stars to reference or indicate periods of time in art, statues, dedications, murals and mosaics. For the ancient Romans, who were essentially at their beginnings, an agricultural society, the seasons and their marking of time through stars and astrology, was vitally important. Personal zodiac signs were also frequently included in charms and amulets.

Astrology also played a part in art and social interaction:

There was a round plate with the twelve signs of the zodiac set in order, and on each one the artist had laid some food fit and proper to the symbol; over the Ram, ram's head pease, a piece of beef on the Bull, kidneys over the twins, over the crab a crown, an African fig over the Lion, a barren sow's paunch over Virgo, over Libra a pair of scales with a muffin on one side and a cake on the other, over Scorpio a small sea fish, over Sagittarius a bull's eye, over Capricorn a lobster, over Aquarius a goose, over Pisces two mullets.

Petronius, *Satyricon*, Chapter 31

As well as practical uses for astrology, the stars did engage the heart and souls of the ancient Romans, just as much as they do today.

If any man cannot feel the power of God when he looks upon the stars, then I doubt whether he is capable of any feeling at all.

Horace, *The Odes*

Nature and the Elements

Stemming from earlier Latine and Etruscan beliefs, in ancient Rome all of nature was deemed sacred, often even deified, as were the individual places and elements *in* nature. For example, rivers were considered deities, such as the river Tiber. That great river that was the life line of Rome and previously known as Albula before it was deified as the God Tiberinus when Tiberinus drowned in its waters.

It was believed that every aspect of nature, such as trees, rocks, soil or streams, also had a resident or protector spirit, genius, nymph or a connected deity, who was to be worshipped, respected and given offerings. Perhaps the most well-known association of a natural element to a deity is Jupiter and the thunderbolt. However, originally the:

> *Etruscan writings take the view that there are nine gods who send thunderbolts... The Romans have kept just two of these, attributing daytime thunderbolts to Jupiter and nocturnal ones to Summanus*
> Pliny, *Natural History*, 2.138

Other examples are the Querquetulanae who were Roman nymphs of oak trees and both Tibernius and Volturnus were both spirits associated with the river Tiber in Rome. The waters of Rome were associated with various naiad's, such as Juturna, Goddess of the sacred spring in the Forum, though she did preside over all fountains in Rome. Her sister, the water naiad Lala (who became Lara 'The Silent Goddess'), by Mercury was the mother of the twin Lares who guarded the crossroads of Rome, watching over all passage to and from Rome. Terminus was the god of the boundary markers, most often stones, that lined farmer's fields. Silvanus was a God that was known to particularly reside in and govern the woods and wild lands. He protected the woods and presided over tree and wild growth.

Pomona was the Goddess of the Orchard and cultivated fruit trees and could be found and worshipped amongst the apple, olive and fig trees. Both the gods Neptune and Fontus were Roman gods of wells and springs. Ascensus was the Roman god of hillsides, Collatina, the Roman goddess of hills and Montinus the Roman god of mountains. Not only could you make offering to these deities in their location but also you would evoke them when passing through their terrain, out of respect and in hopes of safe passage. The residing spirits of a place were respected even when the name was unknown and there have been many dedications on altars found with the words *'to the gods that inhabit this place'*. The Romans were practical and it was better to be safe than sorry!

There were also deities connected to human interaction with nature that required their own supplication when actions were taken that affected or made use of nature. For example, Adolenda was the Roman goddess to whom you would wish to make an offering to before burning a tree, whereas you would want to say a prayer to Coinquenda or Deferunda before cutting down a tree and to Goddess Puta is you were pruning a tree.

The Romans also knew that there were four elements; earth, fire, air and water. Empedocles, a 5th century BCE philosopher from the island of Sicily, is known to be the European origin of the theory of the four elements and also argued that the opposing forces of Love and Strife were the powers that could move, separate and mix the elements. The idea of these four elements was then later used by Hippocrates, Hermes Trismegistus, Plato, Aristotle and Galen, in philosophy, science and medicine. There was also a belief in a fifth element that was considered like movement, or space that could explain the existence of heavenly stars, which it was believed could not be made of the other elements.

Ovid had the elements separated from chaos in this order; firstly, fire flashed, then air came next, followed by earth and lastly water to confine the earth that came before. There were also deities and spirits that were personifications of elements and elemental realms or properties. Caelus was the personification of the sky, Caelum being the Latin word for 'sky'. Sol was the personification or metonymy of the sun and was often depicted with eight rays. Tellus was the personification of the earth and she was depicted as reclining and with fruits or babies in her lap symbolising fertility. Nox was the goddess of the night, Luna the moon and Aurora the goddess of the dawn.

There were also mystical creatures that were associated with certain elements and elemental realms. Ovid shares in Fasti that there were considered to be a hundred water nereids. Fauns were creatures of the earth who were half goat and half human, and they were spirits of the woods and the countryside, as well the nymphs who resided in trees and plants. Shades were considered beings of the underworld, who literally lived under the earth but could visit this realm.

Most often the elements were personified in human form when depicted in art and every day symbolism. A beautiful example is the depiction of the four season who framed the ascending figure of Emperor Titus on his posthumous triumph arch monument in Rome. This depiction and use of the seasons in iconography was often used to highlight the element of time. The same depiction was used on the arch of Septimus Severus where statues of the four seasons stand beneath the flying victories. Emperor Constatine similarly had the figures of the sun and moon on his arch. As well as accompanying Victory as a personification of time, the Four seasons can also be found accompanying the God Saturn, Goddess Pomona, Goddess Flora and Goddess Fortuna, all of whom were considered to be thematically linked.

Philosophy

Woven into the ideas of culture, religion, politics is often philosophical ideas or ideals. This is certainly the case with the ancient Romans whose life and actions were guided by *pietas*, a word which attempts to sum up the idea of duty. This sense of duty was something that was woven deeply into Rome from its very beginnings and could be considered their overall primary philosophical idea, and so it is Pietas we will explore first.

From the 1st century BCE onwards, Roman philosophical thought began to be more readily influenced by the philosophy of the ancient Greeks in particular but they also made their own studies and schools of philosophy. Previously, foreign philosophers had been greeted coldly, such as the ambassadors from Athens who were immediately sent back by an unwelcoming senate in 155 BCE. However, Greek Stoicism and Epicureanism were two schools of philosophy that did became popular in ancient Rome, chiefly because they fit well with the practical and disciplined nature of the Romans.

Pietas

Malo Mori Quam Foedari 'Death rather than dishonour' An Ancient Roman saying.

Pietas could be considered *the* guiding compass for all aspects of life in ancient Rome. Pietas is the Roman idea that every Roman, whether emperor, child, man or woman has their duty towards their country, their gods and their family and friends, both those are alive and those that are dead (ancestors). It was considered chief among the Roman virtues. Cicero defined Pietas as that:

...which admonishes us to do our duty to our country or our parents or other blood relations.
Cicero, *De Inventione*, 2.22.66

Pietas could be considered religious observance in that many rites of passage or daily rituals were dictated by the idea of Pietas and it encouraged Romans to be both respectful and faithful in their observances. It did in fact encourage Romans to be both respectful and honourable in *all* their daily interactions and reminded them of their social duty and to contribute to the community. An example is that it was considered a sign of respect and honour to walk next to an elderly person and act as support. Pietas was speaking with respect and honour to your parents, being kind to a stranger, being honest in your business transactions and diligently remembering your daily offering and praise to your household Lares (spirit).

The Roman hero Aeneas was considered a prime example of pietas. The tales of Aeneas and other heroes, and sometimes heroines, often formed the moral education of children. Stories such as the daughter who suckled her mother to keep her alive were taught from a literary collection of such tales that were compiled by Valerius Maximus in the 1st century BCE. His *Memorable Sayings and Doings* shared such stories such as the devoted daughter as a resource for the moral formation of children and a reminder to adults.

Pietas was also embodied by the Goddess Pietas who represented the divine nature of duty, loyalty and devotion. In the Forum Holitorium stood the Temple of Piety, dedicated to Goddess Pietas which was erected in the 2nd century BCE. Within the temple was a golden statue of a father figure, that represented, and reminded, that the divine that was in all things and all people and so should be honoured. Pietas was also often symbolised by the stork bird.

Honour was also considered a god, and he was the husband of reverence. Their child was majesty.

Chapter 3

Sacred Place and People

*I soon saw that Rome stands out above all cities, as the
cypress soars above the dropping undergrowth.*
Virgil, *The Pastoral Poems*

The Eternal City

The whole city of Rome was and is considered scared. In
ancient Roman times the divinity of Rome was personified by
the deity Roma Dea, the goddess Rome. She was protector of
Rome, sometimes considered a Lares (guardian) or genius of the
city. She was often depicted with, or one and the same as, the
Goddess Virtus, who personified the idea of virtue and could
also be considered the essence or energy of the city.

Rome was a sanctum defined by its seven holy hills and the
river Tiber. Each part of the landscape was sacred, from the river
Tiber which was honoured as the god Tiberinus, to the seven
hills and districts of Rome, each with its own mythology, history,
deities and temples. The seven hills became encompassed by a
wall, much like a helmet protects the most important part of the
warrior. The gates of Rome were sacred gateways or doorways
into this holiest of sanctums and were guarded and protected
by the God of gateways Janus.

Terminus, the Roman god of boundaries, sanctified the
boundary markers and his bust could often be found upon
boundary stones and markers, including those of the city of
Rome, He is often associated with the saying *concede nulli* "I
yield to no one". Due to the divine presence of Terminus a
boundary was believed to have sanctified power to repel and

protect. Rivers were also considered boundaries by the Romans and energetic markers.

Burials had to be made outside of the city because of this sanctified space, as per the Law of the Twelve Tablets, laid down in 451 BCE. The Appian way, also known as the sacred way and the oldest street in Rome, was the principal road leading south out of Rome and became a popular location for burials outside of the city. It became a causeway of tombs and memorials where the dead were honoured, remembered and witnessed on every journey in and out of Rome. The Appian Way itself, however, was also deemed a sacred pathway in and of itself, not just because memorials and burials of the dead began to decorate its sides. Its age was beyond memory and it led to and from a central point in Rome, a monument, known as the Golden Milestone. The saying 'all roads lead to Rome' referenced that all roads in the empire led to this golden milestone.

Palatine Hill was considered the ancestral centre or heart of Rome. In some myths it was the location of the cave of Lupa, the She-Wolf of Rome (and later her shrine) and the original hut of Romulus. For others it was also the home of the hero, Evander. Either way Palatine Hill always represented the city's sacred birthplace. The holy boundary which circled the base of Palatine hill was believed by the ancient Romans to have been the very circular route set by Romulus, that he marked through the Etruscan Rite of Plow in 753 BC. It was this circular route that was reaffirmed, honoured and literally followed every year during the circular run that formed part of the Lupercalia festival. The Palatine Hill remained sanctified through the history of ancient Rome and it seems that no public buildings were built there during the early history of Rome, apart from temples, such as those to Goddess Victory, the God Apollo and to Jupiter. Emperor Augustus did, however, decide to build his royal palace there in 44 BCE.

Capitoline Hill, was second in sanctity and importance, only to the Palatine. It housed the largest temple in Rome, to Jupiter and the Capitoline Triad. Within that temple was the stone or altar of Terminus. It was believed that this stone must always be exposed to the sky and so a small hole was made directly above the altar in the roof of the temple.

Between the Capitoline Hill and Palatine Hill was the Roman Forum, the centre of Roman life and home to the temple of Vesta, the eternal and most sacred flame, that was the hearth of Rome and the Empire. The Forum was located on what was originally a marshy bog and, in the Forum, the sacred spring of the water-spirit Juturna was a reminder of this watery past. Before 700 BCE parts of the Forum were used as the earliest cemeteries, long before burial was banned in Rome's sacred precincts.

Each location in Rome had its associated or protective deity, often represented by a statue, mosaic or painting. At the baths and exercise halls could be found statues and associated symbology of Flora, Hercules, Fortuna and water naiads. At the theatre could be found the same for Baccus and Venus. The Goddess Minerva and the God Apollo, who both were associated with the cities guilds of writers and craftsmen could be found at the libraries and street of book sellers and makers. Minerva could also be found depicted as the patron of crafters in their warehouses/factories, and in medical or healing facilities, along with Jupiter, Apollo, Hygeia and Asclepius. At the amphitheatre and triumphal arches, the God Jupiter held primary place, in the markets and areas of commerce such as the forum and ports, the God Mercury. The ports were protected by the God, Portunus. The house of Juno was also the city treasury and Terminus could be found on roads, and at boundary markers, crossroads and walls, along with Janus. Each crossroad also had a *Lar*, or protective spirit that must be invoked or have an offering made to. Some locations were named after mythological figures such as the Tarpeian Rock, from which the Romans were said to have thrown traitors. This rock was named after the woman Tarpeia who betrayed the Romans to the Sabines in the earliest years of Romulus's reign.

The sacred and deities could also be associated with every aspect of daily life and work. The temple of Juturna, the goddess of wells and springs was also the religious centre of ancient Rome's Water office, from which Rome's water infrastructure was managed. You would hear Fortuna and Mercury invoked in games of dice in the baths or prayers said to the God Tiber when you crossed one of the bridges of Rome. Even the streets and roads of Rome were governed over by deities. Clivicola was the deity that presided over slopes and sloping streets.

The very fabric of Rome was also sacred. The characteristic stone, *tufa* (volcanic rock) that paved the sacred Appian way and other roads and buildings came from volcanoes in the Albian hills, south of Italy. The energy or essence of the volcano god Vulcan, principal deity of the early Latins of these south regions was believed to be held in these rocks.

It was not just the upper land of Rome that was holy but also the underground. Even the sewers of Rome were considered to hold a sacred purpose. They were not just practical but were designed to purify and cleanse the city on all levels, physical and spiritual. As well as waste water being carried out of the city it was known for bodies of criminals to also to be placed in the exiting waters of sewers to be sent out in an almost ceremonial way to purify the city of their crime and presence. Famously the unpopular Emperor of Rome, Elagabalus, had his corpse symbolically thrown into the sewer that led to the Tiber after being publicly mutilated and dragged there.

The sewers were sacred to the Etruscan Goddess, Cloacina (meaning 'to purify'), who was responsible for their smooth running, as well as protecting the workers who constructed and maintained it. Later Cloacina became associated with Venus and her shrine, the entrance to the great sewer, called

The Shrine of Venus Cloacina (Venus of the Sewers) was located in the Forum. There were also shrines around and in the sewers to Oceanus.

The Home

Religious observance was practised everyday by Romans in their *domus* (meaning house or household) and was mostly separate to the official state religion's rituals and sacrifices. Of central importance were the domestic gods, Lares and Penates, who were present in all Roman households. They were believed to be guardians and protectors of the home and its associated buildings. Every home had an altar or *lararium*, to their Lar, the protective household god, which was normally located in the *atrium* or central courtyard. The Lar, an Etruscan word meaning prince, could also be an ancestral spirit and was invoked on important family occasions. Two Penates, protectors of the store house and larder would also protect food and drink and they shared the hearth with the Goddess Vesta. A Genius could be another guardian spirit, particularly of a person or a family or tribe and was also honoured in the home and through daily ritual. Prayers and offerings were made daily to the household Genius, Lares, Penates and ancestors, and included items such as incense trays of food and drink left upon the shrine. The whole family would make these daily offerings, including children. The guardian spirits of the home would take of the offerings what they wished and what was left could be consumed by the family. The Lares and Penates were also especially honoured on the kalends, nones and ides of every month and on these days the household hearth was decorated with garlands.

In *The Pot of Gold*, Plautus, the 3rd century BCE playwright has a household Lares lead a man to discover buried treasure in the house in which they both reside. By doing so The Lares initiates a turn of events that lead to a moral play about being miserly. It links the Lares with luck, chance and the ability to offer blessings upon the household.

In case someone is wondering,
I'll briefly introduce myself.
I am the household God
Belonging to the family you saw me leaving.
I've kept a watchful and proprietary eye
On this establishment for many years now,
For the father of the present occupant
And his before him ...
He has one daughter.
Every day she comes
To pay her respects, and always has
A pinch of incense for me, or some wine
Something, anyway,
And hangs me around with garlands.
Plautus, *Aulularia* (The Little Pot/ The Pot of Gold)

Terminus was another household deity that guarded property boundaries and could protect from intruders. Goddess Concordia may also be appealed to, to bring harmony to the household and the relationships of the people within it.

There were also deities that would support specific household activities, for example, Sylvanus watched over woodcutting, woodcutters and those that worked in the forests and woods. Goddess Pallas was the deity who watched over preparing yarn, weaving and spinning of wool and cloth. Pallas was also the goddess who taught children literature.

An erect phallus was considered a symbol of strength, power and good fortune and was a very popular good luck charm that was placed on buildings of home and workplaces as sculpture, as well as in decoration and ornaments and elsewhere around the household and buildings as graffiti or artwork.

The Forum Romanum

A forum was the centre of any Roman city and was essentially a closed-in marketplace, with a market, shops, cafes and the basilica and was the equivalent our own modern day town hall. The Forum Romanum likewise was at the centre of ancient Rome and the religious, political, legal and commercial nucleus of the city. It heard the great oratory of politicians, saw the burning of the bodies of Emperors and was the location of more than a dozen riots. It was also the location of many of the rites, rituals and ceremonies of the official state religion, with temples bordering it and religious activity spilling out into its confines. Within the forum was what was called 'the navel of Rome', located next to the shrine of Vulcan, and this was deemed by many ancient Romans be the centre of the world.

The Forum was located on the area that was previously marshland, between the sacred hills of Capitoline and Palatine. Archaeologists have discovered that beneath the Forum were several huts and an extensive burial ground that date to the late bronze age and early iron age. By tradition it was believed to be the location of the home of King Numa Pompilius, whom the ancient Romans believed to be pivotal in forming and creating many pillars of the religion of Rome. In the 7th century the Forum was officially formalised, drained of water and paved. A sanctuary and altar were created in the Forum in the 6th century to protect the remains of what was believed to be the grave of the cities founder, Romulus. It was covered with big slabs of black stone and is known as 'The Black Stone'. Later in the 1st century BCE the Forum again was extended outward from this original location by Emperor Augustus.

The forum was home to the *Curia*, where the meetings of the Senate were held and the *Comitium*, an open-air public meeting space for the 'assembly of the peoples' which often witnessed many a prophecy, as well as religious rituals and procession. Within the forum was also the temple of Concord, the temple of Saturn, the temple of Minerva, the temple of Castor and Pollux, the temple of Divus Julius, the temple of Janus, the temple of Venus Genetrix (The Mother of Aeneas), the temple of Augustus and the temple of Mars Ultor. There was also a fountain and shrine of Juturna that, according to the Roman comedic playwright Plautus, drew the sick to drink its miraculous waters.

Also located in this sacred space was the high altar of the Temple of Vesta. If the forum was the heart of Rome, then the Eternal Flame, tended by the Vestal Virgins, was the blood that kept it pumping. It was a temple greatly honoured and many times restored by kings, the republic and then emperors throughout the full history of Rome. No man could enter this part of the sacred precinct.

The Forum was also the location of The Regula, the home of the king and later emperors. Not only this but it was the headquarters for the Pontifax Maximus, the head of the priests. Emperor Augustus attempted to honour the sanctity of the Forum by attempting to enforce the wearing of only formal toga in the forum instead of casual dress.

The Temples

The oldest type of holy place was the sacred grove (a small group of trees or wild garden), many of which had shrines within them. Most were located near, or had within them, bodies of water and were associated with water cults. Offerings were often made and placed within these groves. Sacred groves continued to be used and were important places within and outside of Rome, even when larger temples began being built. Such an example is the grove of Diana, near Lake Nemi. Many temples were also located near, and associated with, specific ancient trees, such as the Sacred Oak Tree of the Temple of Jupiter *Feretrius*. These trees and waters were treated with as much respect and reverence as the temples and gods themselves.

It was very common for most deities to retain a grove as well as a temple, as a reminder of the connection between the Roman gods and countryside cults and agricultural themes. Even lesser Gods and those not associated with fertility, such as *Robigo*, the goddess of blight, mildew and rust had their own groves. There were also groves dedicated to the ancestors and figures of significance such as Romulus, Remus and Numa.

There were also sacred places called *sacrarium*, meaning shrine. Shrines were generally smaller than the larger temples but more prolific. They were dotted all over Rome, and could even be found in homes.

Most temples of ancient Rome were a compilation of native Italic styles, derived primarily from Etruscan traditions of architecture and deity. The characteristics of Roman temple design included a raised podium, columns on just three sides of the temple, with none at the back and most of the emphasis on the front of the temple, with steps leading to the portico (sacred porch) and a single cella (room). Roman temples were only open at the front, with steps on the front side only. Roman temples could be found in both rectangular and circular shapes, with the circle preserving or emulating the circular shapes of the huts, temples and tombs of the earliest occupants of the area. Many have emphasised that the earliest temples were defined by their circular shape, which reflected the circular stone tombs and wooden sanctuaries of the Etruscans, as well as emphasising the sacredness of the hearth as the centre of life. Later in the republic, rectangular and square shapes are also utilised in temple building. Some temples, such as that of Fortuna, had U-shaped altars, though most altars were square or rectangular.

The primary purpose of a temple was to house the statue of the deity and was a sacred sanctum for the priests/priestesses. The inside of a temple was not, in general, a public place and offerings, sacrifices, public rites and rituals were performed on the portico outside and viewed from a courtyard below, or, in the space surrounding an outside altar. Betting, games and gambling were prohibited in the porticos of all temples.

The two oldest temples in Rome were believed to be the Temple of Jupiter Optimus Maximus and the Temple of Saturn (497 BCE), whose altar was believed to have been connected with the founding of the city. Both the shrines of Vesta and Vulcan were considered to be two of the earliest shrines in the city. Both stone and marble were used in temple construction as well as Roman concrete. The first all marble temple was built for Jupiter Stator in 146 BCE. In 82 BCE Emperor Augustus claimed to have rebuilt eighty-two temples in marble, but retaining the classical style.

Many of the temples were commissioned by emperors and nobles, both of these being some of the few citizens that had both the funds, authority and influence to create such buildings. Temples could be built to patron deities, such as the Temple of Apollo on the Palatine Hill, that was dedicated to Augustus' personal patron deity and the Temple of the Unconquered Sun, Sol Invictus, that was built by the emperor Aurelian. It was also common for temples to be built in dedication to past emperors, though many more were started than completed, such as Nero's temple to his deified step-father Claudius.

Some temples were built in dedication to certain events. Such an example is the Temple of Mars Ultor (Mars the avenger) in the Forum which was the grandest temple built by Emperor Augustus. This temple celebrated the victory of Augustus over his assassins in 42 BCE and inside it also housed the standards of the legions lost to the Parthians, as well statues of Mars, Venus and Augustus himself. Another example is the Temple of Peace, added to the Forum of Peace. It was built by Emperor Vespasian between 71-9 CE, following a violent civil war in Rome, to act as a reminder of the blessings of peace. This temple famously housed the Ark of the Covenant that was taken from Jerusalem when it was captured by the Romans in 70 CE.

Before a temple was built it was important that the ground was sanctified. The writer, Tacitus, shares about the rebuilding of the Capitoline Temple of Jupiter Optimus Maximus on 21st June 70 CE. The man in charge Lucius Vestinus:

> *summoned the soothsayers, and they recommended that the ruins of the former temple should be carried away to the marshes and a new temple erected on the same foundations; the gods were unwilling, they said, that the original form of the building should be changed. On 21 June, a day of bright sunshine, the whole consecrated area of the temple was decorated with wreaths and garlands. In marched soldiers, all men with names of good omen, carrying branches of auspicious trees: then came the Vestal Virgins accompanied by boys and girls, each of whom had a mother and father alive, and they cleansed it all by sprinkling fresh water from a spring or river. Next while the pontiff, Plautius Aelianus, dictated the proper formulae, Helvidius Priscus, the praetor, first purified the site by a solemn sacrifice of a pig, a sheep, and an ox, and then, duly offered the entrails to the altar of turf, he prayed to Jupiter, Juno and Minerva, the guardians of the empire, to prosper the enterprise, and by divine grace to raise on high the house of their which human piety had here begun ... on every side gifts of gold and silver were flung into the foundations, blocks of virgin ore unscathed by any furnace, just as they had come from the womb of the earth. For the soothsayers had given out that the building must not be desecrated by the use of stone or gold that had been put to any other purpose.*

Tacitus, *The Histories* Book 4. 53

The day of temple consecration was also often noted in the fasti and in general that day became a feast or birth day for that deity.

The inner chambre of a temple was not a place to gather and worship together as a congregation, nor were public rites completed inside. Often it was outside the temple that such activities as sacrifices and ceremonies were performed. The inner chambre remained the home or house in which the deity resided. On feast days occasionally the statues of the deities that normally resided in the temple were taken out for a parade through the streets of Rome. The extended Temple buildings were, however, multi-purpose with the remains of shops and rooms being found in the basements of many. The portico or colonnaded porch of a temple was also often used for public addresses and speeches.

The decoration of the temple, including screens, statues, altars, arches, mosaics and columns were often dedicated by those that had the means, to display their wealth, status and devotion. This was also the case with regalia and utensils. Many temples had sponsors that would pay for building or maintenance as part of their pietas. The temples had custodians who were called *aedituus* who were responsible for the maintenance and upkeep of that temple. Normally the custodian lived next to the temple or shrine. The term also covered anyone that was involved in the cleaning and maintenance work, this included the slaves that were given to the temple.

King of All Temples

According to Roman tradition the original Temple of Jupiter, the king of all temples, was commissioned by Romulus himself during or following ongoing conflict with the neighbouring Sabines, in thanks for his aid. From the beginning of ancient Roman religion Jupiter was considered Optimus Maximus, the 'best and greatest!' and so deserved a temple fitting to his station.

Capitoline Hill saw the dedication of a Temple of Jupiter Optimus Maximus in 509 BCE upon the site of the original temple. It was the first temple of such a scale in Rome, as it was the size of two Olympic swimming pools. It was typically

Etruscan in its design in that it had columns on only three sides of the building. In the year of its creation Rome saw significant festivals and celebrations for the opening of this first temple of the newly established Roman republic. It swiftly became the principal temple of the city and honoured Jupiter as the source of Roman glory, as well as reflecting the divine mission of conquest and domination that Rome believed it had.

Within the centre it had three inner chambers for each of the Capitoline Triad, one in the centre for Jupiter and one either side for Juno and Minerva. The temple was also said to have a tiny opening in the roof, so that the God Terminus, the God of boundaries who was also honoured in the temple as the original boundary stone, could see nothing but the stars.

Other Temples

Equal in importance to the temple of Jupiter was the Temple of Vesta, protectress of families and the state. Her original temple, which was technically a house, not a temple, was believed to have been built by King Numa Pompilius, one of the first Kings of Rome (8th – 7th century BCE) and it was a circular hut, such as the original homes and shrines of the first peoples of Rome. This temple was home to the eternal flame which was guarded by the Vestal Virgins, her priestesses. The flame was symbolic of the city and as long as it was kept alight the city remained eternal also. Kept under the protection of this temple and its high priestess were several sacred objects including the Trojan Palladium, two Penates statues and a sacred image of Pallas, whom the Romans considered a goddess of the hearth. Aeneas, the Roman's great ancestor, supposedly brought the image back from Troy.

In the house of the vestals were many statues and dedications to high priestesses and also a large statue of Numa Pompilius, one of the earliest kings of Rome and famous for being ascribed with so many of the earliest religious institutions and procedures.

This statue also served as a reminder that this location was the sanctified location of the *Regia*, meaning 'throne room' that was the home of the early kings of Rome. The vestals were originally thought to have been the daughters of the king and tended the sacred hearth in his home. The regia contained a shrine of Mars which may have contained the sacred shield of Mars that was believed to have fallen from the sky into the house during the reign of Numa. The shrine of Mars was a reminder of the connection between Mars and the kings of Rome. He was an example to them, as Mars the father, who was, like a shield, the divine protector of Rome. At the time of the republic, the king of Rome's religious roles and functions were replaced by a high priest that took on the religious authority that the kings had previously had and also lived in the regia. His residence was adjacent to the house of the vestals and this was where he conducted his official business.

At the other end of the Forum from the Temple of Vesta, was another of the oldest temples in Rome, the temple of Saturn and reputably the oldest sacred site in the Forum, its consecration being somewhere in the late seventh BCE. On this site there had been an open sanctuary that dated from the early seventh century BCE, which contained an earlier shrine which legend said had been visited by Hercules on his travels. The temple of Saturn was home to the bronze tablets on which the laws of the Roman state were inscribed.

Kings and Emperors

Both kings and emperors of Rome had religious influence and responsibilities, their position was not just a secular and political role. The original Etruscan cities were mini states ruled by kings, with each state having a patron or affiliated deity. In this trend Romulus was remembered and celebrated as the first king and founding father of the settlement of Rome and his religious preferences set the tone for the religious future of Rome. The mythologies emphasised him as a hero, a descendant of Venus, the son of Mars and a priestess of Vesta and particularly devoted to Jupiter. With all of these references he had an almost demi-divine status that sanctified his actions and in turn the city he built. He himself became the God Quirinalis after his death or ascension to heaven. Following Romulus was the Sabine King Numa who was credited by the Romans with introducing many of the religious ceremonies and institutions of public religion. He was said to favour a muse called Tacita, 'The speechless one' also known as Dea Muta, The Silent Goddess. He encouraged the people of Rome to emulate and worship her by introducing silent reflection and meditation as a religious, political and social practice which would in turn bring about peace. After him Etruscan, Latin and Sabine kings created the forum and then built their greatest ever temple, that of Jupiter, Juno and Minerva on Capitoline Hill, setting the three in stone as the principal deities and Capitoline Triad of Ancient Roman Religion. The God Mars and Goddesses Venus, Vesta and Roma remained popular with the Roman city and connected to the idea of kingship, as well as continuing to be personally connected to Rome's rulers.

Popular religious practices and preference were also marked by a link to the mythology of the Roman kings. In the foundation story of Rome, there is a significant pivot point when Romulus and Remus used augury with birds to decide who would win their rivalry. Augury or divining by nature continued to be a popular religious rite and ritual and though inherited from the Etruscans came to be seen as a principle Roman religious practice. The mythology of the ancestral use of augury only supported its popularity and gave it validation.

The kings were also important in building religious buildings and sanctifying certain sites. Romulus is credited with the first shrines to Vesta, Vulcan, Jupiter and Mars. The early philosopher king of Rome, Numa Pompilius was also attributed with creating (or making official) many of the early Roman religious institutions, founding temples, such as the temple of Janus and was known as the 'law-giver'. The vast religious knowledge that he introduced was said to have been given to him by his lover who was the Goddess Egeria. King Tarquinius Priscus the Elder, Etruscan king, according to legend, built the Circus Maximus with its temples of Luna and Sol in a sacred marking of place of the location of the rape of the Sabine women. He was also believed to have established *the Ludi Romani*; the annual celebratory games held in honour of the God Jupiter. The games were established in gratitude to Jupiter for a successful conquest and continued for many, many hundreds of years later. The kingship of Rome was both a secular and religious role and after the last kings of Rome and into the republic, their specific duties were still performed by one man, a priest, whom retained the term rex (meaning king) in his title but was now the subordinate to the High Priest of Rome. He was called the *rex sacrorum*, and he performed acts, rites, rituals and worship that were still deemed important to perform to keep equilibrium with the divine, but could no longer be performed by a king.

After the end of republic, the emperors reformed the kingly tradition of being both political and secular leader and priest. Never more so was the ruler priest as well as head of state, than in the reign of Emperor Augustus. In the reign of Emperor Augustus, the rulers of Rome began being treated as divine. It was a quick turn-around, however, as Marcus Anthony, second in command to Julius Caeser, had only recently been mocked as losing his Roman *Virtus* for being hailed as a manifestation of the God Baccus in other parts of the empire. From leader to slave a Roman man was expected to be dignified and restrained and not led to outward displays of extreme pride or arrogance. Despite the condemnation of Marcus Anthony, not long after, Julius Caeser was the first ruler to be deified by priests and the practice continued with rulers that followed. The essential difference was that Julius Caeser was deified *after* death and any attempt to claim divine status while alive, such as the case of Marcus Anthony, was considered tyrannical. Later in Roman history Emperor Nero was shunned for claiming that he was an incarnation of the sun god Helios and it was seen as a sign of his unsuitability to rule.

The first deification of a ruler, that of Julius Caeser, was in part to give legitimacy, authority and splendour to Augustus. He encouraged, perhaps even instigated this deification because if Julius, his uncle was deified then the shadow of his light would also fall upon Augustus himself. A temple was built in honour of Julius Ceaser in the forum with his comet decorated statue inside.

Despite the earlier resistance to deify emperors in their lifetime, many emperors were worshipped by their subjects all over the empire, not just in Rome. To get around the problem of not being deified in one's lifetime, Augustus allowed his subjects to worship at altars and temples of his *genius*, which was a term used for guardian spirit or divine aspect, or the *numen* of the emperor, numen also meaning divine power or essence. This could be equated to worshipping the archetype or idea of the emperor, rather than the emperor himself.[6] Dedications, offerings and sometime worship were made to the Numen Augusti, or the divine nature of the emperor, and it became part of the official state religion6. In his lifetime he remained *divi filius*, son of God, rather than God himself.

Augustus was, however, named a God by the Senate after his death and it was noted how from his funeral pyre his soul flew to heaven in the form of an eagle, a sure sign of his divinity. From this time on the genius of the emperor was intrinsically linked with Roma Dea, the goddess of Rome and, by association, also loyalty to Rome. The resulting imperial cult led to the worship of the imperial numen and the deification of popular emperors after death. The cult of the emperor and the worship of dead Emperors at their associated temples, also became a branch of the cult of ancestors. Perhaps in humour, resignation or hope the emperor Vespasian is said to have joked on his deathbed 'Oh dear, I seem to be becoming a god!'

It is also argued that unification of emperor and religion was an attempt to unify the empire, which contained many gods, beliefs and practices, under one ultimate authority that was both religious and secular in nature. During his lifetime Augustus was pivotal in determining the religious splendour and responsibility of future Emperors of Rome, as in his reign he was successfully able to marry religion and propaganda, politics and religious ritual. He determined that every emperor from then on had a degree of religious responsibility.

Other politicians and leaders often also had religious roles or work experience. A young Julius Ceasar was a priest of Jupiter and later, he served as Pontifex maximus, chief priest. He was not alone in this.

The personal relationship of Emperors and kings with deities is also noted by their contemporaries. For instance, Tacitus describes a time when:

[Emperor] Nero went to the Capitoline Hill to consult the gods about a journey. He worshipped the Capitoline gods [Jupiter, Juno and Minerva], then entered the Temple of Vesta. Suddenly all his limbs started trembling. He was frightened by the Goddess. Or perhaps he was frightened, remembering his crimes. Anyway, he abandoned the journey."
Tacitus, *Annals* XV 36

Trajan on his triumphal arch at Beneventum is shown depicted with Jupiter. This companionship was intended to fuse hero and God and lend the godly radiance of the supreme to his subject. Apollo was known to be the favourite deity of Emperor

Augustus. Emperor Tiberius was noted for his worship and favour of Goddess Concord and built a temple for her after his triumph over Germany. Marcus Aurelius was known to be a member of several cults, including that of Glycon, the Divine Snake and was initiated into the Eleusinian Mysteries. Nero favoured Apollo and even had himself depicted in statuary as Helios and Apollo with a golden diadem on his head. His Palace was also known as the Palace of the Sun (the sun being Nero himself).

The Goddess Aequitas was also associated with the emperors. She was the goddess that was the personification of equity and presided over fair dealing. Sometimes as Aequitas Augusti she was worshipped as an aspect of the emperor. Fecunditas Augusta is a Roman goddess who was associated with the empresses of Rome. She was the personification of the fertility of the empress and the hopes of the empress bringing forth and raising children. She was also a reminder of the importance of the Empress as a primary example to all of Roman of the *Mater Familialis*.

Soldiers and the Roman Army

Janus, Jupiter, Mars, Pater, Quirinus, Bellona, Lares, Divi Novensiles, Di Indigetes, Gods who have power over us and our enemies, and You Manes, to You I pray, I venerate, I ask your divine favour and beseech You, that You prosper the virtuous might and victory of the Roman people, the Quirites, and upon the enemies of the Roman people may You afflict them with terror, fear and death. As I have pronounced the words, even so on behalf of the Republic of the Roman People, and of the Army, the legions and the auxiliaries of the Roman people, do I devote myself and with me the legions and auxiliaries of our enemies to the gods of the Underworld and to Tellus Mater.
Marital, *Epigrammata*, 8.2.8

In the Imperial age Rome was a military state and the soldiers made up a huge proportion of the population. Although they would have shared much the same upbringing and general religious experiences of roman citizens, they also had their own allies and affiliations, expressed in a way that was specific to their role and sometimes to the land in which they were stationed. The principal deity of the roman army was Jupiter Optimus Maximus. Jupiter Optimus Maximus, as the patron God of the army, was erected an altar as an important annual military ceremony. He remained the constant principal deity of the army, an army whom it was believed he founded and governed. However, soldiers within the roman army seemed to have also favoured the gods Janus, Mithras, Sol Invictus and Mars, as well as the Goddess Roma, and the Goddesses Victoria and Bellona, who both aided men at arms. Sacrifices to the emperor were also compulsory and worship of the emperor was a sign of loyalty to Rome Several goddesses appear to been associated with war symbolism, including Juno and Fortuna. However, under the *Pax Romana* Juno and Fortuna were celebrated as the concepts of protection and guardianship rather than associated with actual warfare. Bellona in contrast was considered *the* Goddess of War, and was present in battle bestowing ferocity and courage as well as supporting with battle strategy.

Bellona was venerated by citizens and soldiers of Rome alike as the Goddess of battle, conquest, as well as bloodlust and strength. She protected the homeland and she was your go to for battle logistics and warfare tactics both at home and away. She was actually Sabine in origin and was mostly worshipped and venerated solely for herself. However occasionally she was represented along with Mars or Jupiter. In her cult, led by her priests, the Bellonarii, she was associated with *Virtus*, the personification of valour.

The military would declare war by visiting the temple of Bellona, located in the campus martius. Inside was a symbolic area of ground that represented the enemy soil, into which they would throw a sword, spear or javelin to signify that they were initiating war on that enemy. The first noted instance of this happening was in 280 BCE. Her temple was known as the official military decision making centre and foreign ambassadors, not allowed into the walls of the city of Rome, would be allowed to stay in the temple complex.

Arguably the roman army had the most exposure to foreign gods, through the conquering, then settling of frontiers and also the signing up of locals to the army, from those newly occupied regions. This was reflected in the popular worship of Greek and Persian Gods and heroes within the army. Many Roman solider tomb dedications can be found that express devotion to both local cult gods and the roman pantheon, as well as the genii loci of the land in which the soldiers were stationed. A frequent occurrence was the romanisation of foreign gods. This was either to ensure their protection of the roman army, and, or, to ease integration of that culture and its associated religious cults, for the overall stability of the army and to ensure continued loyalty. Such an example is Mithras who was a Persian God and found great popularity within the roman army and can be found depicted with his Persian symbols but in roman dress and style. His worship was often conducted in temples that were constructed like, or built within caves, a reference to the cave where Mithras killed a bull. He was popular with soldiers because he was a God of triumph and the battle of good and light over dark and evil. The Greek hero Herakles and his symbols were also popular, as were the Egyptian God Serapis and the Hittite God Dolichenus. Under the Emperor's reigns many new provinces were acquired and the roman army began to consist of few Roman citizens but more often nationalities from outside Italy, who also would have retained their own religions. Yet, no matter the country of residence for a legion, the roman army as a whole retained some universal religious alliances, notably the oath of allegiance to the Emperor and the God Jupiter.

There was also symbology and reference to the divine in what the soldiers wore and used. The eagle of Jupiter was *the* symbol of the roman army, and his lightning bolts were also used on shields. The *aquila*, Jupiter eagle, was the standard carried by a high ranking or veteran solider and it symbolised the military might of Rome. It carried the honour of the entire army. The *imago*, a portable bust of the emperor, was also carried by the legions, as a reminder to legion of their oath of loyalty. More than the technical advances of warfare, weapons and armour, the attitude of the roman army with regards to *Virtus* – loyalty, courage and discipline - is what made it so affective. It was believed to be Jupiter that inspired this virtus.

The legions also took their emblems from gods and goddesses. They could be found upon the individual standard of each legion. Pliny the Elder in his *Natural History* lists four principal animals that were used; wolf, eagle, boar and horse. The wolf was a protective symbol of the God Mars Pater (Mars the Father), the eagle of Jupiter Optimus Maximus and horses were connected to Mars and with Neptunus Equester, God of horses and horsemanship. The 20th Roman Legion, Valeria Victri is an example that had a boar as its emblem. Boars, like the horse, were symbolic creatures that spoke to the agricultural history and traditions of the roman people and therefore also the ancestors. The boar, was also a reminder of the rural pastime of hunting and connected to both deities and heroes, such as the God Silvanus, the Huntress Diana, Ceres and later when Greek Myths became popular, also with Hercules. All four animals were symbolic of the particulars strengths or gifts of on an associated god or genus and their use hoped to endow or inspire that legion with either tenacious ferocity (wolf), stubborn determination (boar), victory and pride (eagle) or nobleness and heroism (horse). The second legion Augusta, raised during the war that bought Augustus to power honoured him by taking his emblem, the Capricorn (a mythical sea-goat), as their own. There were also aspects of the army that connected to the mythology of Rome. For example, Plutarch shares that a company of soldiers called *manipulares* was named for a particular band of man that carried poles tied with shrubs and hay in the legend of Romulus and Remus (Romulus, 8, *The Rise of Rome*).

The roman army also carried various religious items with them as they travelled across the Empire. These items could include good luck charms given by a loved one or portable shrines and altars. The portable shrines acted as an altar when stationary but with a door which could be opened and closed as needed and kept a statue safe inside during travel. It was also common to have small portable altars for burning incense offerings upon.

Within every *principia*, or legion's headquarters was the *aedes*, which provided administration offices, the strongrooms, a space for military ceremonies and housed the regimental shrine. At the shrine were displayed the legion's standard, as well an altar to the gods as well as a statue of the emperor. This space was considered the sacred heart of the principia and revered as such. The punishment for defiling this space was severe. The Campestres were guardian goddesses whose role was the protect the parade ground and military camps of a roman fort or military enclosure. They seem to have been favoured mostly by cavalrymen. A strict calendar of rites and rituals were associated with the regimental shrine and the cult of the emperor. When needed the roman soldiers themselves acted as the priests, with the commanding officer presiding and, just as in society in the city of Rome, men simultaneously held offices of both priest and secular roles/ work.

Within the army it was also known for the rite of the *devotion* to be used. The devotion was a sacrifice, one that was taken by a military general, or a substitute solider in his place. This sacrifice was made to gain the favours of the gods in battle and so turn the battle to the romans favour. The sacrifice was made as a vow, in which he vowed himself and the enemy's army to the Goddess Tellus and the gods of the underworld. He would offer his own life, that the gods would take in battle and in turn would grant the army victory. The life of the general or solider could however but substituted with an image of themselves, which would be buried after the victory. This ritual was mostly to demonstrate the faith, devotion and courage of its general and so inspire his soldiers.

Priests and Priestesses

A priest in Rome was called a pontiff (pl. pontifices) which literally translates as priest. Those priests who were particularly working for one of the fifteen principal cults of Rome were called the flamen (pl. flamines) of that cult. Other priests and priestesses included the augurs, the vestals, the Sibylline, the epulones and the haruspices.

The office of 'flaminate maiores', the major or head priests of the principal gods (Mars, Quirinus and Jupiter) remained exclusive to patricians (the Roman elite), however, by 300 BCE around half of the regular pontifices were plebeians. From 104 BCE regular pontiffs were selected by popular election. For the majority, to be a pontiff was not a profession nor a full-time job. One exception to this were the Vestal Virgins who lived and worked as priestesses for a thirty-year contract. Despite it being a part time job, a man remained a pontiff for life. Being a priest did not affect a man's legal rights and they could still become *paterfamilias* (head of a Roman household), get married and have children. The majority of priests were male, however, there were priestesses for some of the Goddesses, such as the Vestal Virgins and a few for male gods. Jupiter, for example, had two priestesses. There were also some cults that were restricted to women, such as that of the Goddesses Pudicitia and Bona Dea.

The role of priest was not as we would consider one today. They were not an intermediary between the gods and the people, nor were they professionally concerned with the spiritual welfare of the people. Rather, they facilitated the worship of the gods and administration of state religion including; advising the senate on religious matters, supervising religious law, determining the date of festivals and organising the celebrations. Sometimes they would only be involved in the organisation and running of one annual festival, such as in the case of the Luperci priests at Lupercalia, and this may be all that their role entailed.

The office of temple keeper could also be given as a gift, such as in the will of Claudia Quinta who gave her guardian the position of temple keeper or servant for Diana, to secure him in his old age. The role of temple servant could involve meeting, greeting and looking after visitors, assisting priests with ceremonies and processions (such as playing music or singing and carrying standards) and acting as site security with jobs such as gate locking. There were also temple clerks and interpreters. Slaves were also bought and given to the temples as workers and were then owned by the temple until they were freed. They performed services such as cleaning, collecting and distributing materials to be burnt such as wood and serving food and drink at the feasts and festivals.

By the late Republic (3rd to 2nd Century BCE) there had been four major priestly collages created. The priestly college called the *Titii* was named after the Sabine King of Rome, Tatius, who co-ruled with Romulus. His successor Numa is credit with introducing the priestly college of the *Fetiales* whose purpose was to ensure justice in war and to bring about peace. He is also said to have established a flamen of Quirinalis, who was a priest dedicated to the divine Romulus. The *Salii* were the priests of

Mars and were known for their war dance with shields performed during the month of March. By the time of Julius Ceaser there were fifteen primary colleges of *flamen*, one designated to each area of Rome and their associated deities. For example, the *Portunalis* with the flamen of the God Portunus, God of the harbours and the *Pomonalis* the flamen of Pomona, Goddess of the orchards. There were three major *flamines* devoted to the principal gods; The *Flamen Dialis*, devoted to Jupiter, the *Flamen Martialis*, devoted to Mars and the *Flame Quirinalis*, devoted to Quirinus. Additional to these three were twelve minor flamines which included the Portunalis and Pomonalis, as well as the *Carmentalis* (Goddess Carmenta), *Cerialis* (Goddess Ceres), *Falacer* (God Falacer), *Floralis* (Goddess Flora), *Furinalis* (Goddess Furrina), *Palatualis* (Goddess Palatua), *Virbialis* (The God Virbius and Goddess Diana), *Volcanalis* (God Vulcan), *Volturnalis* (God Volturnus) and one other who is unknown. The office of 'flamen' or 'flamines', which might be translated to "he who is cloaked" or "he who burns offerings/ makes sacrifice" was an ancient one, who origin was in obscurity but was believed to hark back the pre-republic times of the Roman kings. When outdoors flamen priests would wear a distinctive apex headdress; with involved a close-fitting felt cap, covered by a disc like ornament with the apex on top. The apex was a pointy stick of olive wood. The emperor had his own flamen who could sacrifice on his behalf. The wife of a flame was called the *flamen dialis*.

Often, prominent or important Romans sought out priestly roles or functions. Achieving a priestly role or status could afford political advantages and standing which in turn would affirm status and could offer the ability to be one of influence. You would often find those hoping to rise in the political ranks at some point gaining 'religious work experience'. The men that had priestly roles would take part in rites, rituals and ceremonies when needed, and return to their normal life when not. When in 'priest mode', such as during sacrifice, the toga would be lifted and positioned over the head to mark the sanctity of time and place. It was believed that to draw the toga up over the head acted as a barrier or boundary of sacred space, that would keep out sights and sounds of ill-omen. The Romans shunned the Greek practice of worshipping or performing ritual with the head uncovered as they found it disrespectful. There was one exception to this Roman trend and that was with the worship to the God Saturn, whom received sacrifice with head uncovered, so that it was open to his benign energy and blessing. Pure white linen robes were the chosen dress for priests and priestesses, or anyone who was taking part in an official ritual. The vestal virgins had distinctive headdresses that were also recognisable and had a defined religious uniform.

At the top of the priest hierarchy was the *Pontifex Maximus*, the head of priests, whose name meant 'the great bridge builder'; he who was a bridge between the divine and the people. The pontifex maximus was in charge of the state religion and his role was to oversee and supervise the work of most of the priests and priestesses, including the vestal virgins. By the republic he was elected to his position and his role incorporated some of the duties of the earlier kings of Rome. Julius Caeser held this office during his life and it greatly benefited his political career. Augustus was the first Emperor to become the Pontifex Maximus while Emperor. The traditional continued after Augustus with all subsequent emperors.

The *augures* were another important body of priests and were those that officially observed the flight of birds in order to divine the will of the gods. This was a priestly order and practice than was inherited from the Etruscans and there were sixteen men that performed this role. Cicero was one politician to hold this office and he wrote about many of the practices and observances involved in his literary work 'On Divination'. Related to the *augures* were the *haruspices*, meaning "gut-gazer".

This college of sixty priests, governed by the chief haruspex, were those that carried out the divinatory practice of haruspicy, which divined though interpreting the entrails of sacrificed animals. They were respected as interpreters of the will of the gods and again had their origins in Etruscan practices. Another divining priest was the *fulgurator*, who interpreted lightning.

There were also the *uates*, which Wiseman translates as 'bard',[7] which were those that would orate or profess predictions, had supernatural knowledge and chanted oracles. Their role was to speak the words of the divine if and when they were inspired to do so, however, they were also directly consulted and by peoples of all levels of society and office. They were sometimes to be found orating and chanting in the Roman Forum. Other *uates*, such as the Sibyl priestesses kept to shrines, temples or seclusion. Ovid, as a poet and historian, names himself an uates in his book, *Fasti*. Carmentis, the goddess of prophetic song was invoked by uates. Carmentis was also the name of the high priestess of the Cimmerian Sibyl, either as a derivative of her name, or in honour of Carmentis, the mother of Evander the epic hero of Roman mythology whom was believed by some to be the first Sibyl of the Cimmerian.

The Sibyl of Cumae, were priestesses of Apollo and part of a Greek colony near Naples. There were believed to have originated with the original Sibyl (meaning prophetess) herself, a demi-god that was blessed with prophecy by Apollo and gave her name to her priestesses, just as Vesta did with her Vestals. The Sibyl was traditionally said to be nomadic but finally settled in an underground cave near Cumae. The priestesses were blessed with the sight of prophecy and were unofficially consulted several times during Rome's history, though their relationship with Roman authority and priest cults could be strained and conflicted. They were known to use a mixture of sounds and words to share their visions. Collections were made of their sayings and predictions and could be consulted by people of any level or station. The Sibyl of Cumae were also said to protect a book of oracles that was believed to have been created during the time of the earliest kings of Rome and offered to the last King Tarquin. It was the consultation of this 'book' that led to the acquisition of the great stone of Cybele and her following inclusion into the Roman pantheon.

Vestal Virgins

Arguably the most important and certainly well-known of the priestesses of Rome were the Vestal Virgins or the 'Cult of the Hearth'. Cicero even meant so far as to say that 'if the gods did not hear the Vestal Virgin's prayers, the state would not survive'. The Vestals were an order in devotion to the goddess Vesta and whose history goes back before the Romans to ancient Latium and Etruria. Rhea Silvia, the mother of Rome's founder Romulus and daughter of the King Numitor was said to have been a vestal virgin and it is thought that the Vestal virgins were a continuation of the very ancient practice of the king of Latium's daughters tending the hearth in the palace.

So vital were the Vestal's to the maintenance of Rome that the rules governing them, from their selection to their everyday life, were strict. During the time of ancient Rome, the six vestals were chosen between the ages of six and ten by the Pontifex Maximus himself. The girls could be from any rank of citizen, including the daughters of freedmen (ex-salves). Aulus Gellius lists some of the requirements for selection:

> *Her father and mother must be alive; she must have no speech impediment, hearing-defect or other physical weakness, and her father must not have surrendered his legal control over her.*
> Gellius, *Attic Nights* I 12:1.

Once selected they were required to serve as vestals for thirty years, after which they had the freedom to choose to leave or stay. Most decided to stay and the longest living Vestal that we know of, Junia Torquata, served for 64 years. During their time as a Vestal, they were expected to remain chaste and serve in complete devotion to Vesta and the Eternal Flame of Rome. It was their task to keep the flame burning. As long as the flame remained Rome would not just prosper but survive and so their role was both sacred and vital for Rome's very existence. There were six vestal virgins and they took it in turns to guard the sacred flame.

Included in their role was the creation of Mol Salsa, a sacred offering of wafered wheat, that was used by both the Vestals and the people of Rome. They were also involved in some religious rituals of the state, including those with other deities other than Vesta. An example of this is that they oversaw the sacrifices in the mysterious female only rituals of Bona Dea (Goddess of fruitfulness). The rituals and ceremonies, which did involve strong-wine, dance, music and blood sacrifice in her honour were participated in only by married women and were hosted both publicly at her Aventine temple and privately for select matrons of the Roman elite. As Bona Dea was the Goddess of Chastity, and due to the exclusion of men in the rites, it was appropriate for the vestals to lead and supervise the secret rites and festivities. Bona Dea, like Vesta was also a protector of Rome and the two cults were connected.

To be able to fulfil this important work they lived in the house of the Vestals, called Atrium Vestae, which was located in the Forum Romanum, next to the circular temple of Vesta. They had the luxury of their own garden and bathing facilities, as well as servants. They were greatly honoured and very well respected, receiving a large dowry from the state and the privilege of being accompanied by a *lictor*, a bodyguard or attendant. They were also gifted the ability to reprieve any condemned criminal and their voice did have a place of authority. This is demonstrated in the case of Empress Messalina who appealed to the Vestals for support when she married her love Silius. It was noted that the head of the vestal virgins, Vibidia, spoke for Messalina and asked that she not be condemned before she was able to speak in her own defence and her request was granted.

The vestals enjoyed banquets with the powerful and influential and were the only women that could travel in a carriage in Rome, other than the Empress. They did not have to swear an oath in court as their word was completely trusted and respected. They also had the ability to create a will and manage and dispose of their own property. However, if they broke their vows at any time, such as letting the fire go out or breaking their vow of chastity, they would be sentenced to death either by being whipped or buried alive in an underground chamber.

In the central court of the house of the Vestals there was unearthed by archaeologists several honorific inscriptions, along with busts of the head priestesses. These remains give us insight into the way in which the Vestals were honoured and respected. One inscription reads:

To Flavia Publicia, the most devout and sacred head of the Vestal Virgins, who after passing through every grade of the order and serving the altars of all the gods and the eternal flame, with pious mind day and night, deservedly succeeded to that office in the fullness of time.

Chapter 4

Rituals and Tools

With these words the goddess must be appeased. Say
these words four times turned to the east, and wash
your hands in living water. Then, having set up a vessel
as if it were a mixing- bowl, you can drink snow-white
milk and red must, and soon with nimble feet fling your
vigorous limbs over the burning heaps of crackling
straw.

Ovid, *Fasti*, Book 4 April 21st

Ritual was important in ancient Rome as it offered a point of
connection to the divine and because it was believed to keep
universal equilibrium. Rituals, offerings and sacrifice were
made publicly on behalf of the Roman state and people, and
privately as a contract between an individual and the divine.
The Performance of public rites was all important and strictly
on time and in the right place as rituals decided the destiny of
Rome. The words used in both private and public rites were just
as important and forms of address and invocation were strictly
adhered to. If part of a ritual or invocation went wrong; it would
have to be repeated from the beginning again or be considered
a bad omen. The correct form of name and appropriate epithet
must also be used for the deity as it was believed that a deity
would not respond to a prayer if they were addressed incorrectly.
Sometimes this was avoided by using the phrase *or whatever*
name you wish to be called after the deity was named. Dedications
were also made to 'the unknown god' when it could not be
determined whom the thanks, ritual or offering was for and you
did not want to offend by using the wrong name. Ovid also uses
the useful phrase *all you gods whom it is dutiful to summon* (Ovid,

Fasti, Book 4). Plutarch shares another rule that was by tradition given by King Numa in his introduction of religious regulations in the 8th century BCE. He laid down the rule that *to the gods above sacrifice an odd number, but an even number to the gods below* (Numa. 14. *The Rise of Rome*). Ritual prayer was made with the hands lifted and the palms of the hands facing upwards. This was the case for all the gods, except for those of the underworld when hands and arms would be facing down. *Carmen* were any rhythmic or poetic words, saying or formula, such as epitaphs, spells, prayers, hymns, oracles and oaths, that were said. Jupiter Lapid was the god whom presided over all solemn oaths and he was associated with the lightning struck stones that sometimes were used to swear solemn oaths upon.

It was not believed that the gods were obliged to answer prayer or request. However, it was believed that the gods were more likely to respond to requests if an offering or sacrifice was made and ritual formula adhered to. In most prayers to the deities, it was Janus, Mars or Jupiter that was always invoked at the beginning as an act of respect and a hint to their primary status. In early Rome and the republic Vesta was addressed last in all prayers and rites, as at the end of speech the offering would generally be given to the fire. However, from the time of Augustus it seems to have changed that Vesta was moved to the beginning of the liturgical order of address.

Let us now explore some further aspects of ritual, and ritual tools and offerings.

Statues

One of the most well-known survivors of ancient Rome is its statues and it has been joked that in ancient Rome there were more statues than people! This may be partly down to the fact that sculpture survives so well but is also testament to the significance and use of sculpture in ancient Roman religion and devotion. Contemporaries of the 1st century BCE record 3,785 bronze statues and 154 decorated or made with gold or ivory, as well as many more terracotta and wooden pieces. Statues were made depicting deities, emperors, ancestors, spirits and high-ranking nobility. Many adorned public spaces and temples and were used in ritual.

Though they favoured terracotta or wood in the majority, the Etruscans were well known for their bronze statues and their bronze statues were much prized by many surrounding cultures. In the late republic, the bronze artists remained almost exclusively Etruscan, however by this time, coloured stone had also become fashionable and was more readily available to all levels of society. Later still when the influences of Greek styles and artists began to be adopted, white marble become the most common material used for statues. It is believed from analysis that many of the often-white sculptures that survive today would have originally been painted and so the gods and goddesses would have been brightly coloured and would have looked almost life like. The remains of paint help us to determine the sacred colours associated with the deities.

The statues of deities would grace the roofs of temples, as well as the inner sanctum and portico of the temple. They were also in significant spaces and places around Rome, such as crossroads, the Forum, bridges, arches and roadsides. Busts, or portrait heads, of deities and emperors, were also common in Rome and the Roman style of realistic and dignified portraiture was very popular. Roman sculptures of significant persons in general gave more focus and central importance to the face of their subject. Many Romans also kept death masks in their homes for the worship of ancestors.

Smaller figurines of deities were also used as more personal depictions of the gods in household altars and shrines. Sometimes these figurines were even small enough to be hand held.

Procession

A religious procession was a very common occurrence in ancient Rome. It often was the opening event to a festival, games or races, in which the statue of the associated god or goddess would be taken through Rome to an area of celebration. It was expected that as it passed, all who viewed the statue were to rise to their feet out of respect (or fear of causing offence). Particular observance was made to the patron god of a person's profession or organisation. Often included in the procession, following the deity statue, would be the sculpted images of dead emperors and then sometimes the living Emperor himself. Lamps and torches were lit and lined the roads, and the procession was often accompanied by the music of pipes and flutes.

Another example of a procession was the Triumph of the army after a successful battle. The commander would lead a triumph, or procession, and would begin by entering the western Triumphal gate. They would then cross the Campus Martius (the field of Mars), circle Palatine Hill, before passing through the forum and completing their sacred way at the Temple of Jupiter on Capitoline Hill. It was a procession not only to celebrate the general and his army but also to thank Jupiter for their success. Jupiter's symbols were part of this procession, with an eagle topped ivory spectre being held by triumphator, as well as a laurel wreath and olive branch. The solemn procession made its way to Jupiter's temple for sacrifice and a ritual was conducted to give thanks for the victory. White sacrificial oxen were part of the procession and the priests would sacrifice the animal and catch its blood as part of the follow-up ritual. The procession also included *ludiones* (Etruscan dancers), horn blowers and foreign captives.

The triumphal route itself eventually became lined with many monuments and statues over time and it was also used by Emperors as a ceremonial route on other occasions. By tradition the first triumph through Rome was enacted by Romulus after his first victory in battle against King Acron. Thereafter the ceremony, route and symbology were linked to the mythic and semi-divine founder of the city. Interestingly the first triumph was also believed to have been held by Romulus on 1st March, and honoured Mars his father and Jupiter *Feretrius* (Jupiter that smites). This date became the first day of the first month of the Roman calendar and the first day of the military campaign season. Romulus was believed to have made the first triumph on foot and later King Tarquinius made the first triumph by chariot.

Divination

Divination was a popular form of prediction and of interpreting omens. Divination could be used to determine political and military decisions, as well as those for personal matters of business and life. The respected *Augures*, divinatory priests, most often Etruscan (even in the later Roman period) would perform three different types of ritual observation; hepatoscopy, prophecy through oracular tools and augury, and the observation of natural phenomenon, such as bird flight and weather. These three principal divination tools of ancient Rome all had their origins in Etruscan divination, where they were used as a staple of Etruscan religious practice. The most notable portents that were divined were noted in the annual *fasti*, or religious calendars.

Hepatoscopy was used by the Etruscans and Romans by examining the liver or entrails of a sacrificial animal. They would sacrifice the creature in ritual and then examine the liver for signs and premonitions. Clay liver models possibly served as a guide for priests. The model would help them to consider the shape of the liver and whether it could signal a certain outcome to a situation or question. Certain areas of the liver corresponded to different deities and various possible answers to questions. An important archaeological find is the Etruscan model liver, which is marked with the names of deities on each area of the liver in relation to their exact region in the sky. The Etruscan god of lightning, Tinia, had his region due north and if lighting struck there or north east this was considered a good omen, while north west lightning was interpreted as bad. Therefore, if there was a blemish in the north east region of the liver model corresponding to Tinia it could be interpreted that he did favour the action, sacrifice, intention or decision that had be made and it must be changed or altered in some way. It is assumed that this model liver was used as an instructional tool for those learning divining.

Augurs would divine through the use of physical objects, such as knucklebones, counters and even opening a book at a certain page or word. Particular attention, however, was paid to nature. Observing nature as divination would involve noting and interpreting acts of nature such as storms, earthquakes, lightning or the movement of fire or water. Any of these phenomena could be a message, warning or scolding from a deity or an epiphany or manifestation of one. Priests were taught to learn and interpret the difference. For example, the place where lightning struck the earth was deemed as sanctified space and often marked as being a site which was bestowed with the presence of Jupiter and therefore belonged to him. This form of divination also included the behaviour of animals and birds; three birds flying north and upwards would mean something very different to four birds flying south and downwards. According to Plutarch the bird that the augurs paid most note to was vultures. This was because these were the birds that Romulus saw flying over Palatine in his dispute with his brother Remus over the location of their city, as well as the vulture possessing mystical qualities in themselves (Romulus, 9, *The Rise of Rome*). Plutarch also shares that Numa would only take on the mantle of kingship once a sign from the gods, in the form of birds, was witnessed. It is noted by Livy and other writers that many a Roman battle only went ahead due to the favourable behaviour of a flock of sacred chickens, kept solely for the purpose of affirming the gods favour or disfavour of military tactics.

Gaius Umbricius Melior was one of the most celebrated haruspices in ancient Rome. He was employed by the emperors and wrote a book on divination in the 1st century CE. He was buried in a tomb built at public expense.

Offerings and Sacrifice

Offerings and sacrifice were important to ancient Romans as it was believed that they were needed to keep equilibrium between humans and gods. If the priests maintained the order of public sacrifice and ritual then it was believed that the gods would in turn protect the city of Rome and its people.

An offering could be made either with a request or be given after a request had been granted. After a deity had granted a favour, it was usual for a grander offering to be made than the offering that accompanied the request. A grand offering would be such as an altar, created as a way of saying thank you for favour, fortune and success. Altars were usually dedicated to a single deity, either by groups of people or individuals. You will find upon most Roman altars an inscription that includes the name of the deity it is dedicated to, the request or aid that they granted, followed by the people or person who dedicated it.

When any offering was made, to any deity, it was important to first make an offering of incense and wine to Janus, God of doorways. In Ovid's *Fasti*, Janus explains that this must be done:

...so that through me, the guardian of the threshold, you can have access to whichever gods you want.
Ovid, *Fasti*, Book 1, Line 174

A common way of making any offering was to burn them upon an altar. Upon the surface of most altars was a hollow (called the *focus*) within which a fire could be lit to burn offerings such as cakes. Burning offerings was common because it was believed that *devouring fire purges everything* (Ovid, *Fasti*, 21st April). The offering was received by the deity through them smelling or inhaling the fumes, the smoke raising up to them in the heavens. Other offerings were buried, thrown into water or sanctified ditches/pits, placed around the footings of buildings. The location would sometimes depend on the deity to whom you were devoting to. Offerings given into the earth were often to earth-connected deities or those of the underworld such as Tellus or Orcus, and fire for the upper world or heavenly gods such as Jupiter or Juno. In general, beneath the earth and in water were both considered sanctified spaces and appropriate places for objects containing divine energy as it put them beyond human consumption or use. Ovid shares that both water and fire were popular offerings, tools of ritual and receptors to offerings *since in these is the cause of life* (*Fasti*, 21st April). Offerings could also be broken or bent as a way of offering then to the gods as it deemed them unusable in this world.

Offerings could range from the bones, ashes and blood of sacrificial animals to flowers, crops, wine, oil, precious metals, milk, jewellery, totems, statues, lamps and coins. These offerings could be used in combination or on their own. For example, during the foundational ritual in which a boundary stone was sanctified and dedicated to the God Terminus, crops, flowers, and wine were all offered into the foundational hole, upon which a stone was then placed. Yearly this ritual would be repeated but with the difference that in repetitive years the crops, garland of flowers, wine and sometimes sacrificial blood were placed upon the stone, rather than under it. This annual ritual offering was accompanied by hymns, song and feast in honour of Terminus.

Bronze tablets with dedications inscribed were also offered to a temple and its deities. After the burning of the Temple of Jupiter in 69 CE the priests searched in vain for three thousand lost tablets that had been given at the temple and kept in storage. A common phrase that was used and inscribed on dedications and invocations was 'VSLLM' or *Votum Solvit Laetus Libens Merito* meaning 'Paid his vow, gladly, freely and deservedly.' Dedications were considered not just nice words, but contracts and official record.

Milk and honey were both suitable as offerings as they were considered the gifts of the gods and reflected the sweetness of life. Milk was sometimes used as representative in place of the divine breastmilk of the goddess, such as in the case of the festival of Lupercalia where milk anointed on the forehead of participants represented the life-giving milk of the She-Wolf Goddess. Libations of milk, instead of the normal wine, were also made to Rumina, the Goddess of breastfeeding and child rearing. Ovid shares that honey is offered at new year as an offering to Janus:

> *...so that the flavour may follow what ensues, and the year continue sweet on the journey it has begun*
> Ovid, *Fasti*, Book 1 187-188

Honeycomb is noted by Ovid to be a common offering, especially in rural rituals and celebrations. Honey was also used in medical rituals, rites or offerings associated with healing.

Flowers were a very common offering, especially to the Goddess. Apuleius writes of a ritual where.

> *The procession of the saviour goddess began. Women in white robes, with wreaths of spring flowers on their heads and arrayed in jewels, scattered petals on the ground.*
> Apuleius, *The Golden Ass*, XI 9.

Roses, rosemary and violets seems to have been particularly popular flowers. In fact, what could be considered consumables, such as flowers, crops, incense, salt, wine, and food stuff, such as grapes, bread, cake, fruit were the most prolific of offerings, with dried dates, figs, roses and rosemary are specifically mentioned as the most common plant offerings. These items were a personal way of displaying faith or asking for favours and used very often in personal rather than public ritual. They were items widely available to most Romans but this did not lessen their value. Offerings, such as jugs, plates, altars, statues, were given to temples by wealthy worshippers. Ovid also notes in *Fasti* that in the grove of the shrine of Diana at Nemi *"the long fence is draped with hanging threads"* (269) and so cloths and 'ribbon' were offered at sites, just as we still tie ribbons to branches near springs and in woods today.

Plutarch shares the Roman tradition, that it was considered protocol to sit after one had made an offering or act of worship. To do so was to indicate that the blessing had been granted and the prayer accepted, as well as to offer a boundary or threshold that marked one sacred act from another.

Animal Sacrifice

By Roman tradition, in the times of Romulus and Numa, the first two kings of Rome, all sacrifices were bloodless. King Numa was in particular celebrated by writers such as Ovid and Plutarch as ruling that sacrifice *"ought to remain pure of any kind of killing"* (Plutarch, *Numa*, 16).

However, from the time of the Republic archaeological evidence suggests that animal sacrifice was central to rituals and worship of the Roman pantheon, with bulls and pigs being used in particular. There were quite strict rules surrounding the animal that was deemed fit for sacrifice and it had to be unblemished, with no marks, or deformity. Historians have also concluded from dedications that it seems that male animals, such as bulls were sacrificed to the Gods and female animals, such as cows, were sacrificed to the Goddesses.

The animal sacrifice would begin with burning incense and the animal was adorned with garlands of flowers and its horns gilded. Then it was taken to the entrance of the temple and there, wine was often poured upon the animal, as well as fragments of Mol Salsa. Then bristles were taken from the centre of its forehead as a first offering and burnt in the altar flames. This was followed by slitting the throat of the animal and the blood that flowed was collected in *paterae*, golden saucers or bowls, depending on the deity.

Sometimes the whole carcass was placed upon a pyre as offering. Other times after the sacrifice, the entrails of the animals were used for divination and various parts of the animals were burnt as offering, often first covered in sacred oil. Then what remained was eaten by the priests of the deity or sometimes also those taking part in a larger ceremony and banquet. The most important parts were always given to the deity but it was normal for the rest of the meat to be consumed in feasts or redistributed to the general public. This sharing of the meat was often the only source of such food for the common populace and feasts and sacrifices contributed to the feeding of the masses.

The most prized sacrifice, and of highest value, was the bull, being the most precious creature in the ancient Roman world, as it pulled the plough. White sacrificial bulls/oxen with gilded horns were particularly offered in worship, thanks and request to Jupiter and Mars. Regular bulls were also offered to Mars, Apollo and Neptune. Cows were sacrificed as offering to Juno and Minerva. The skulls of oxen were also believed to ward off evil and often buried underneath buildings, or sacred spots and even used as decoration in friezes and reliefs for this reason. It was typical for any purification ceremony, such as that for the consecration of a temple, to include a triple sacrifice to Mars, which included a pig, a sheep and an ox/bull. Other animals were also sacrificed such as goats, pigs and sheep. Domestic fowl was a common offering to Mercury.

For those that were poor and could not offer animal sacrifice, flowers and cakes were also acceptable. Flowers and cakes could also be offered for daily or regular rituals and animal sacrifice kept for important occasions, such as to ward of natural disasters, or plague, or for a special feast day or to celebrate a returning army or the assession of an emperor.

It may be that animals also played a part in temple iconography and symbology. Many deities had associated animals that personified characteristics of the deity or were somehow connected to them in their mythology or epiphanies. Such an example is the live geese of Juno, one of her most sacred birds, that were kept and honoured in the city of Rome. They, like herself were considered great guardians and their death would have been seen as a disastrous omen for Rome. The remains have also been found of the lioness skins that were used to decorate Cybele's altar precinct. Her holy lions symbolised regal status and female power.

In some temples there were strict rules against using animal products or sacrifice. For example, it was forbidden that anyone should wear leather or other forms of dead skin in the temple of Goddess Carmenta, so that dead material could not defile the pure altars.

Human sacrifices were not a part of Roman religion or religious practices and many Roman writers voice a strong opposition to it and condemn it in other cultures.

Votives

Another form of offering was the votive – items that are created or made with the purpose of using as an offering. For the sick, votive offerings were made of the area that was infected or needed healing, such as model arms, legs and eyes. It is believed that this was to make it very clear to the gods where and what to heal. It has been argued that it is possible that anatomical ex-votives were also given as a thank you after healing had already occurred, or, as part of a person fulfilling a vow to a deity. These votives were made from a variety of materials, from bronze and terracotta, to stone, marble, gold and wood. Decorative paint has also been found on the remains of some votives and hint that some Romans went to great expense to decorate votives and, or, to make them anatomically correct. Others were rough and cheaply made. There were often models of dogs, an animal associated with healing and healing deities, found in shrines, temples or near water (water, an element that was considered divine and healing in itself). There was also votives that were objects such as axes, spears, jugs and cups but in miniature. Broches and votive jewellery were also common. Also found given as offerings with or alongside votives are coins, pottery vessels and figurines.

Votives were often offered to specific deities, both major and minor, whom it was believed could assist with a particular area, theme or part of the body. These deities were often considered to specialise in healing. It has been argued that a votive of two silver ears given by a worshipper to Minerva was an offer of gratitude for either a healed physical hearing complaint, or alternatively, as she was the Goddess of wisdom and craft, that the votive was a thankfulness for greater understanding having been gained, or, for learning or hearing what was needed. Temples and shrines associated with Mars tend towards votives in the shapes of hands and feet, reflecting the primary patronization of Mars and his temples, by farmers and those that worked in agriculture. For Mercury, God of Travellers, votive legs have also been found at his shrines and Diana, items associated with childbirth such as votives shaped like vulvas. Votives were frequently sold at shrines, sometimes mass produced and they could be bought outside of most temples.

Libations

Wine was very commonly used in ritual and as an offering to deities. Spring water was also used to cleanse, purify and offered as a libation. Other libation liquids included milk, blood and oil. A *patera* or pan, was used for the ritual pouring of water and blood during religious ceremonies, as well as jugs for water, oil, milk and wine.

Large amounts of wine were offered as a libation in particular to the important Roman agricultural deity, Liber. It was also known for the last of any good wine to be thrown onto the floor as an offering to the gods, especially at the end of banquet or feast. Pure, undiluted wine was used for almost all libations with weak wine the sole drink for most Romans and drunk daily outside of ritual and ceremony. This weak wine still might be poured as a libation at the end of a meal if that is all that could be afforded. Drunkenness was considered vulgar and lacking the Roman *dignitas* and wine in general was honoured, not wasted in this way.

Libations were also a common offering made at tombs, burials and on family altars. In some cases, libation pipes or holes have been found that took wine from above, down into the actual burial. Food, drink, oil and blood were made as offerings to the dead and were believed to contribute to a blissful afterlife. Wine was also used while sharing a meal with ancestors on particular feast days and to placate those passed so that they did not return as ghosts.

Sacred Foods

Olive Oil

It is not an understatement to say that olive oil was the fuel on which ancient Rome survived and thrived. It was used for cooking, oil for lamps in temples and homes, and as an offering, raw and burnt. It was also used in the bathhouses for cleaning the body.

It was sacred to the Goddesses Minerva and Pax (Goddess of Peace) but used in ritual, ceremony and offerings for many deities, including Ceres, Liber and Libera.

Mola Salsa

The ancient Romans used Mola Salsa, 'Bread for the Gods' as an offering. It was used in sacrificial meals, in rituals, placed upon sacrificial animals and on the altars. It was made in bulk by the Vestal Virgins and combined flour and salt and water from a sacred spring that had not touched the earth in its transition. They would use it as an offering to burn, by placing it in the holy flame of Vesta. They prepared it in particular for the festivals of Vestalia, Lupercalia and the Epulum Iovis.

Curse Tablets

It also seems that it was popular amongst the ancient Romans to use curse tablets, which were similar to votives but with different intentions of revenge and punishment, rather than healing. It was believed that the gods might bestow vengeance on request and these tablets were an appeal to divine justice. They also remind us of the perceived role of the gods in encouraging moral behaviour and punishing immoral actions. The vast number of tablets that have survived gives us curses, called defixio, or plural *defixiones,* written on lead or clay tablets, that were hung on walls, thrown into water, springs, shrines or buried in the earth. (Other tablets of requests and prayers were kept by the priests and archived almost in catalogue form. Curse tablets were not). The most common curses are aimed at thieves and asked either for vengeance or seemed to bargain with gods for the return of lost or stolen goods. It was deemed extremely important, as with all addresses to the gods, to get the wording correct and it can be seen that forms and formulas were used that often sound like legal terminology. Sometimes the curses were written back to front, and many included what we would call curse words. It was likewise important to specify and name the god you were appealing to. Curse tablets include many addresses to Jupiter Optimus Maximus, Nemesis and Mercury (God of thieves), as well as local deities and spirits of particular places (such as where the crime happened and was witnessed by the presiding genius loci). It was also common for the gods of the underworld to be called upon to take action, the curse tablets beseeching these gods were often buried or thrown down a well.

Chapter 5

Beliefs and Ideas

Hope is the pillar that holds up the world. Hope is the dream of a waking man.

Gaius Plinius Secundus, known as Pliny the Elder
(23 CE – 79 CE)

Relationship with the Divine

The relationship of the ancient Romans with the divine could be defined by two terms; *pietas*, the devotional relationship between humans and the superior divine, which is a consequence of *religio*, which refers to the cult of the gods with its corresponding rituals.

The Romans knew that the gods were involved in all areas of daily life and were present everywhere, from flowers to doorways. In general, it was believed that the public worship of the divine was transactional and practical; with the divine providing a service in exchange for offerings. Prayers and sacrifices regulated the relationship between the divine and humans and festivals offered a framework for devotions and communication. Tacitus writes about this relationship, sharing that:

...the gods care little for our wellbeing, but greatly for our proper chastisement
Pliny, *The Histories*, Book 1. 3

The goodwill (*pax deorum*) of the gods was of vital importance and was kept through discipline and devotion to observances. Divine favour was the result of virtue and neglect of the appropriate observances could lead to disfavour and misfortune. The Goddess Flora in Ovid's *Fasti* shares about the anger of the gods when supplication and appropriate offering is not made:

Often by sinning someone has made the gods hostile, and there has been a soothing sacrifice to pay for the transgressions. Often, I have seen that Jupiter, already meaning to hurl his thunderbolts, has checked his hand after a gift of incense. But if we are neglected, the offence is paid for with great punishments and our anger goes beyond that just limit.
Ovid, *Fasti*, Book 5, lines 299 – 304

However, the relationship with the divine could also be believed to be one of trust from the humans, and guardianship from the divine. Juvenal, the Roman poet, shares in this vein, that:

the gods themselves know what is good for us and what will be serviceable for our state; in place of what is pleasing, they will give us what is best. Man is dearer to them than he is to himself.
Juvenal, *Satires* 10, 340-350

Perhaps we can presume that for many, the belief in the gods was a matter of mind, heart and soul and a relationship that was as unique as the person that held it. Often, ancient Romans seemed to have had a patron deity, one that was particularly favoured or honoured by the individual. For example, many poets claimed Venus as their muse and writers devoted their works to Venus, Apollo, Jupiter and Juno. Who your patron deity could be, was also sometimes dependant on your trade, family traditions or affiliations or the area you were from. For example, craftsmen would often favour Minerva, the Goddess of craft, or Mercury the God of transaction for those in trade, and farmers may have made supplication to Faunus, Mars, Ceres, Pomona or Saturn.

Roman relationship to the divine was, however, very much facilitated and moulded by the state. Devotions to a deity were made on behalf of the state and the people in public ceremonies and were conducted by state officials (the priests), or, in devotional service, such as that of the Vestal Virgins. The devotions and practices that were made on behalf of the people were often sacrifices, divination and ritual offerings. Religious festivals and temples were both also state funded. In ancient Roman religion there were no religious dietary taboos that we know of.

On a personal level the Romans communicated with and honoured the gods through vows and prayers, evidence of which has survived on altars, dedications, curse tablets, letters, and funerary imagery. Gifts or votives were often given to a deity when a wish or prayer was fulfilled. Romen men and sometimes women wore signet rings with carved stones or gems, called *intaglio*, placed upon the centre that acted as a seal. The images upon these stones frequently depicted deities, and could be a display of a particular preference or patronage of a particular deity. Some rings of soldiers, for example, depict Jupiter's eagle, perhaps in a hope that he would offer his protection to one of his own soldiers and preserve their life in battle. Jewellery such as rings, amulets and hair pins were all ways for the individual Roman to display their personal devotions and to have a private point of connection with their favoured one. Hair pins have been found with images of the sun, moon, Ceres and Minerva. The representation of the divine was a constant in Roman life, with public daily rituals, offerings connected to daily activities and exposure to their images on the reverse of most coins, to hundreds of statues that decorated Rome and the mosaics upon the floors of house and public buildings alike.

Pietas, respect and honour of one's ancestry, country and family, was also important for the ancient Romans and governed many public and private religious actions. For Rome as a whole, Jupiter and Juno were considered the divine king and queen of Rome but Venus and Mars, the divine Mother and Father, and the relationship and veneration with and of them reflected this.

There were many sceptics who argued that religion in ancient Rome was political, with the state religion only being maintained to control or appease the masses, or even control the lower classes. This was believed especially so towards the end of the republic, into the imperial age. Despite this, practices, rites and rituals continued and funerary inscriptions, dedications and personal items still display genuine hopes and devotions.

Genius and Soul

There is something impious and base about rejecting the divine essence of human virtue.
Plutarch (46 – after 119 CE)

There were Romans that believed in the soul and others that did not. There was the same variance as to whether the soul was immortal or only personalised by a human lifetime. The politician Julius Ceaser and the writer Horace are examples of those that openly argued strongly against the immortality of the soul. However, many did believe that there was an immortal aspect of humans that did continue after death. Plutarch when talking of the divine essence of humans shares that:

this comes from the gods and returns to them – not, however, together with its physical body but only when it is entirely released and separated from its body
Plutarch, 28. *The Rise of Rome.*

The ancient Romans also believed in the presence of a genius during one's lifetime. The literal translation of the Latin is 'begetter'. Genius means guardian spirit or divine aspect; everyone and everything has a genius. So, there can be a genius of place or person. You have a genius, so does your home, a tree and your family, school, business and pet cat. Other terms that are similar are deva or essence. An example of genius is the god Tiberinus who was the genius of the river Tiber. In Roman mythology Tiberinus was a very ancient son of a king of Alba Longa who drowned while trying to cross the mighty river. His spirit or soul became guardian god of that river after his death and his soul resided there to protect it. In this instance this genius would be called a *genii loci*, a protective spirit of a certain place or location (not person or animal). A genius, including genius loci, was often depicted as gendered, either male or female and this was shown by their dress, hairstyle and pose in the depictions.

During his lifetime Emperor Augustus was encouraged by some to publicly declare his own divinity but instead he made the politically safer move of suggesting that his genius be worshipped rather than himself. The cult of emperor thereafter was centred around honouring celebrating and worshipping the genius of Emperor; the genius of an idea, concept or archetype and energy. However, it was still common for the physical being of various emperors to be worshipped, despite attempts to prevent it.

It was common practice for the *genius* of the household father and the *Iuno*, or Juno of the housemother to be worshipped. These were not the individual souls of the living and breathing mother and father of the house, but rather an archetypal essence. The genius and iuno were the household primary masculine and feminine symbolic energy of the family unit. The genius and iuno would be contained within the current mother and father as long as they lived, and then passed into the next generation. For example, Gaius Julius Caeser, as head of the 'tribe' or family of Caeser held the genius of the Caeser family and on his death that genius would have passed to his successor and great nephew, Gaius Octavianus Ceasar (later named Emperor Augustus). The iuno of the Caeser household similarly would have been within Julius's wives, entering upon marriage into the family and passed to her successor after death (or divorce).

The genius could also represent what we may call our highest self and a personification of an individual's divine nature. It therefore could define our personality and influence one's desires, needs and actions. The individual genius was honoured by each self, especially on one's birthday. For humans the male soul, highest or divine self was also called genius and for women it was called iuno. In art a Genius and Iuno of a person was sometimes depicted as the image of a snake or a bird and traditionally a person's soul was believed to be located within the head of an individual, hence the preference for, and honour of, memorial busts, in which the spirit could enter and reside if wanted.

Ancestors and Lineage

It is the fate of all good and just men to receive more praise after their deaths than when they were alive
Plutarch, *Numa*, 22

The ancestors were greatly revered and honoured by the ancient Romans. Both ancestors and land had a central influence on the idea of identity and belonging and the cult of the ancestor underlay much private and public ritual. Lineage was important and emphasised in both written word, iconography and religious practices and beliefs.

There are two important Roman ideas to explore in relation to the ancestors; Mos and Pietas. *Mos* was tradition that was passed down and adhered to. Cicero sums up *pietas* for the ancestors and lineage of Rome in his words:

> *Fatherland is the place one's native cults, and the place where one's ancestors are buried, but the Roman fatherland is the one for which we give our loves when necessary.*
> Cicero, *Natural Laws*, 2.2.5

By the time of the end of Republic and into the imperial age, to be Roman was to honour not just the ancestors of your own background and lineage, but also no matter where you were in the empire, to also honour and respect the ancestry around the idea of Rome and its nucleus city.

In the city of Rome, *Mos Maiorum*, meaning the customs of the ancestors, were held as an ideal to aspire to. Ennius writes in *Annals* that "*The Roman state is founded on the morality and men, of old*" (Ennius, Annals, 156). We can see this in the continuation of some ancient practices and festivals, that by the time of the Empire many Romans no longer knew the origin of but still held as important. Long after it was understood why they did what they did, the Romans continued to honour ancestral rituals, rites, ceremonies and festivities in replication of the pietas of heroes and forefathers such as Romulus, Numa, Evander and Aeneas. Aeneas was believed to be the ultimate example of the importance of honouring your city, your people, your family, as well as how to create legacy. In Rome dynastic pride was important and especially emphasised by the leading aristocracy. Julius Ceaser claimed ancestry from Venus, through Aeneas, in order to justify his elevation to Caeser and many noble families also claimed to be descended from the first kings and settlers of Rome, as a point of pride and validation.

The images on Roman coins were one way in which Roman magistrates commemorated the achievement of family ancestors. They also made mention of significant names and events on temple, buildings and statue dedications or on the *fasti* (religious calendar). Horace argues that it was poetry that was the ultimate offering to the ancestors and would secure their immortality. Augustus created a memorial in the Forum to the greats of the past, displaying statues with dedications from Romulus to Julius Ceaser, in testament to their great deeds and achievements.

This pride was also connected with how they honoured the dead, and the use of death masks in ritual, ceremony and funerals brought forth the presence of the deceased. The presence of the death masks served as a reminder of the need to preserve the *dignitas* of the ancestors and emphasised the importance of leaving a good legacy of one's own. To live honourably and with dignity was in itself an important way to display this devotion and honour of family. The ancestors were present in the funeral through their masks and image, as a reminder that they were present and always watching.

It was also believed that dead ancestors could haunt and even taunt the living and so must be appeased.

Forefathers are said to have come out of their graves and complained in the silent night-time, and through the streets of the city and the broad fields they say misshapen spirits howled, a phantom crowd. After that the omitted honours are restored to the tombs...
Ovid, *Fasti*, Book 2, lines 552 – 556

Paternalia was the festival of the Ancestors, held from 13th February to 21st and emphasised the importance of the ancestors to the ancient Romans. These nine days saw the Romans taking part in rites and rituals to celebrate the *di manes* (the dead) and for many, specific family ancestors. The festival began with public ceremonies including the *dies parental* (ancestral days) that was publicly conducted by a Vestal Virgin. Following this there was nine days when no business or weddings took place, even the temples were closed except from those involved in the rites of Paternalia. This was an important part of appeasing the dead so that they would not haunt the living. Statues or death masks of the dead were displayed in the household as a reminder of legacy and honour, and to inspire both. The statues or shrines to the household spirits, or *Lares*, were also cleaned and decorated. Offerings made to the Lares and the dead at this time could include salt, flowers, bread, wine and grain. The festival concluded with the *rite of Feralia* on which offerings were left at the tombs of the ancestors to appeal to those past and ask them to continue watching over the living. There are even descriptions of families having picnics and banquets near the tombs in order to feast with their ancestors. Ovid shares a ritual that was conducted during this time by the Pater Familias:

At midnight the worshipper arises. His feet are bare; he makes a sign, his thumb between closed fingers, in case some bodiless spirit should meet him through the silence. He washes his hands in spring water; he turns, takes up black beans and throws them away, his face averted. As he throws, he says: 'These I cast. With these I purify myself and my own.' He repeats this nine times, without looking back; the spirit is thought to gather the beans, following behind, unseen. Once again, he touches water, clashes bronze and asks the spirit to leave this house. Nine times he repeats: 'Ghosts of my fathers, go forth.' Then he looks back, believing he has duly carried out the rites.
Ovid (1st Century BCE) *Fasti* V 429 – 444, where he is discussing older Roman religious practices

Death and the Afterlife

The gods conceal from men the happiness of death, that they may endure life.

Marcus Annaeus Lucanus, known as Lucan (39 CE – 65 CE)

The ancient Roman views of the afterlife were as diverse as ours. There were those such as the Stoics and Epicureans who expressed disbelief in an afterlife. Julius Ceaser and the philosopher poet Lucretius both did not believe in an afterlife, Cicero also shares his uncertainty, though the historian Tacitus is more hopeful. However, in general, the ancient Romans did believe that something existed or happened after death. This is evidenced by funerary dedications and art that show that there was some universal understanding and general perspectives that influenced burial and funerary practices. Most commonly believed was that there was an afterlife or underworld for the soul and the majority made sure to follow traditions, rites, rituals and ceremonies, just in case. There were also mystical sects in ancient Rome, such as the Pythagoreans who believed in metempsychosis, the reincarnation into an animal or plant.

What comes across as extremely important to the Romans was creating reputation and legacy that would outlive the end of physical existence. To be remembered by the living was immortality. It was likewise deemed to be important to die well, with the comportment of a true Roman, that is, with dignity and honour. Often suicide was seen as a more dignified or honourable way to die, than to be killed by another, such as in the case of Seneca the Younger. Nero's suicide is an example of the opinion that sometimes death was the only way to avoid dishonour. Suicide for personal reasons, other than to retain honour was not considered in the same light. Marcus Antonius was looked at with scorn because it was believed his suicide was a result of his love for a woman. *Damnatio memoriae*, in which the Roman government condemned the memory of a person to eradication was something to be greatly feared.

In ancient Rome child mortality was high and disease, childbirth complications and injury less treatable than today. Therefore, the threat of death would have been a daily companion to the ancient Romans. Many Romans believed that illnesses were caused by the anger of the gods and a religious or magical cure may be sought to reinstate harmony between divine and human. People would also make sacrifices and dedications to a healing deity, such as Apollo, God of Healing and disease, or Bona Dea, goddess of healing and fertility. They may also visit shrines to seek a cure, such as the three temples of the Goddess Febris, Goddess of fevers. Malaria was one of the biggest causes of death in ancient Rome and her temple would be visited by those with fever, who would perhaps also wear a protective amulet against the disease. Seneca describes Goddess Febris as shrewd and honest and many would seek her favour and that of her daughters. Her temple on Palatine Hill was said to date back to before the republic, to the time of Romulus and was said to be located near his original hut. Another on Caelin Hill was founded in the 510 BCE, the first year of the republic. The goddess of health was called Salus, who was worshipped alongside the Goddesses Fortuna and Minerva. Salus had her temple on the Quirinal Hill in Rome and she had many cult wells as well as a presence in thermal baths. She was named Goddess Valetudo, Goddess of military 'hospitals' by the Roman army.

Our first written source for the ideas of death in ancient Rome is that of the historian Plautus (c.250 – 184 BCE). In *Mostellaria* he gives us a glimpse of an afterlife that has stages and levels, some that involve tortures for wrong-doing. He also shares in *Captivi* that there was a societal belief in ghosts and that the ancestors, if honoured, could work in the favour of the living but if neglected could cause major disruption (Mostellaria lines

499-500 and Captivi 998-9). Some souls were also not permitted to enter the afterlife, for example, if they had not been buried and would forever roam as ghosts. Virgil, in Aeneid, also emphasises the importance of having honour in death and correct tribute. His hero, Aeneas, is heartbroken when he sees the many that are stuck lost and abandoned on the entrance to the underworld because they have not been buried.

The writer Catullus describes death as a perpetual night. In his poem 'Death of a Sparrow' Catullus laments the death and the end that comes to all: "*Shame on you, you shameless shades of Orcus, who take what is precious, reduce it all to ash and urn*". (Poem 4)

For further insight we can also look to the Etruscan beliefs of the afterlife to see what most determined the main character and themes of death in the ancient Roman world. For the majority it was believed that it was to under the earth that all souls went after death. Some believed that the soul would reside near the burial, other expressed a belief that the body and soul returned and reunited with Tellus Mater, Mother Earth. From Etruscan funerary art, symbology and remains we can see that the underworld, both in Etruscan and Roman tradition, could be accessed through caves in the earth, as well as through tombs which imitated the cave opening into the earth, and through specific bodies of water (such as Lake Avernus). Another viewpoint was that the soul continued to reside in the tomb, the 'house of the dead', hence the interest in furnishing and filling this eternal room with goods and art. Either way for the Romans the underworld, or afterlife, was believed to literally be under the earth. That the afterlife was considered literally in the underworld is also emphasised by the fact that offerings to the underworld deities were not made upon altars like the other gods, but were buried in pits. Alternatively, it was put forth by some that the otherworld was at the other side of the sea or ocean and the symbology of this was shared through the inclusion of shells and dolphins in funerary artwork.[8] Whether across the sea or under the ground it was generally believed that there was just one underworld for all, and no separation of some souls in heaven and others in hell. Despite this one location for all, some would have better or worse experiences of his afterlife as a result of their earthly behaviour and choices.

The Etruscans, and later the Romans, believed that the afterlife mostly reflected in monochrome the land of living and that in the afterlife a person kept their name and appearance much the same as when living. The collective dead were known as the *Manes* which emphasised the belief in a continuation of personal identity, as well a part in the whole. The *mane* was considered the spark of life of each person, that while living resided in the head of a person and left the body out of the mouth through the last breath (much like one's genius, though genius would return to the divine essence or source after death, or continue through family lineage, while your mane would go to the afterlife). After death some manes could become Lares, guardian of a family or place. For most souls it was believed that they could only leave the underworld during specific times of the year, such as during the festival of Lemuria.

The idea of the afterlife being a reflected version of life is shown in the inclusion (or the painting of) of grave goods in Etruscan tombs which gave the dead person all the amenities they may need, such as food, clothes, pets, armoury and utensils of beauty, eating and recreational activities. However, there are epitaphs that make it very clear that death was considered a rest from or ending of work and labour. The earlier depictions of the afterlife in Etruscan tomb art seem to show a fairly positive experience in the afterlife, with much of the same activity experienced in life. Though some historians have argued that the feasts depicted are actually depicting part of the funeral activities to celebrate the dead by the living, rather than an afterlife scene.

There is a notable change in Etruscan afterlife ideas from the 4th century BCE onwards as the Etruscans begin to be dominated and, in some ways, destroyed by the now well-established culture and people of Rome. From here on there seems to be some terrifying and unpleasant aspects of the afterlife depicted in funerary art, which perhaps reflect the persecution that the Etruscan people felt. An Etruscan underworld deity of this time was Charun, who was a blue skinned monster, associated with snakes and wolves and he carried a hammer. He would guide the deceased into his underground realm and is depicted on many Etruscan tombs with his winged companion Vanth, they were both greatly feared. Other Etruscan underworld gods include the later god Aita, who himself seem to borrow aspects from the God Calu, Calu also being the name given to the Etruscan underworld itself. Both are depicted in Etruscan art with wolf and snake features and symbology, both of which were primary animals that were associated with death and rebirth. In the case of the wolf, for the Etruscans it also had associations with the primary entrance the Roman underworld, the cave.[9] There are also Goddesses of death and winged female creatures depicted in Etruscan tomb art.

The Romans did not share with the Etruscans this idea of death daemons; however, they did believe in the idea of afterlife judgement and the idea of being punished or rewarded for your deeds in life. For the ancient Romans it was the God Orcus, also known as the God Dis (whom we now call Pluto) that was the primary God of the underworld and death. He was also the punisher of broken oaths and God of Wealth and riches, who governed all the resources and abundance that is in and under the earth, such as gold, rubies, diamonds. The Etruscan and Roman Goddess Mania, was a Goddess of Death who was believed to be the mother of all Lares, as well as the undead and ghosts. Offerings were made to her on the 11th May during the festival of Lumeria, a festival of the dead. She was considered a frightening goddess, whom some Roman parents used to frighten their children with. It was the Goddess Mors who was considered the personification of death itself and Goddess Nenia who was the Goddess of the dying and those mourning and whom presided over the lamentations sung at funerals. Apollo, is in his role of the God of disease, plague and the rebirthing sun was another deity with connections to death. Mercury was also associated with death. As the God of travel, it was believed he could guide and facilitate the journey of the afterlife, or into the underworld. The Romans also honoured the Goddess Libitina, who presided over the sacred rites of the dead (some Romans associated her with, or as, an aspect of Venus). Some cults and colleges associated with deities and their worship, also offered burial provisions for their members, such as the cult of the Goddess Diana, the *cultores Dianae et Antinoi*. Apollo, Tellus Mater and Bacchus were all very popular deities as decoration on sarcophagi.

The *Di Inferi* was a term used for the collective underworld gods and goddesses, whom had their own celebration called the *Ludi Taurei*, that was held every five years. Often this collective term of 'underground gods' was used instead of naming them individually. This was done to avoid using their names, which would in turn invoke them or draw their attention, something that was not encouraged.

Not all ideas of afterlife were the same throughout the ancient Roman period. By the late first century CE the Roman poet Decimus Junius Juvenalis writes in one of his satirical poems that:

Today not even children... believe the nonsense about ghosts, underground kingdoms and rivers, with black frogs croaking in the Styx, and thousands of corpses rowed across a tiny boat.
Juvenal, *Satires* III 149-152

However, there was still much ritual, superstition and rites surrounding death and traditions were still followed, even when one did not believe in the afterlife. It was traditional for a close relation to try to 'catch the breath' of a dying man's final breath with a kiss. The eyes of the person would then be closed and all those present would say the name of the person who had died. The body was then washed, clothes and presented in the atrium on a coach surrounded by flowers, wreaths and candles. Typical funeral flowers were Roses, the flower of the underworld.

Burial was forbidden within the sacred pomerium, or city boundary, as made law by the Twelve Tablets of 451 BCE. Therefore, burial was conducted outside of the city and traditionally located along the edges of outgoing roads, especially the Via Appia. Wealthier Romans could, of course, afford larger memorials and family mausoleums were built, mostly in the Etruscan style of a circular building covered by a conical roof, covered in earth and often planted with trees to create a grove. Family members were commonly buried together in these tombs. If not properly buried it was believed the ghost of the person would remain unsettled and so public burial was important and undertaken[10]. Mourning was regulated to be a ten month period and this was the length of time one was expected to be a widow before remarriage[11].

Politics and Religion

If you must break the law, do it to seize power: in all other cases observe it.
Julius Caesar (100 BCE – 44 BCE)

In ancient Rome politics and religion, secular and spiritual, were frequently interconnected. Religion was very much a responsibility of the state and the priests would perform ritual on behalf of Rome, its rulers and people and for political and economic reasons.

In the routines of politics, religion was woven into political decision making, from the creation of laws to elections. Before making important decisions or actions, officials would go to augurs, who would look to signs, warnings and premonitions in nature for answers to their questions. Also, the senate, made of six hundred members, would often meet in a temple, and not only because there were the largest indoor spaces in Rome. Meetings were noted by contemporaries in which they met in the Temple of Jupiter and the Temple of Goddess Concord in the Forum, both whose particular themes of kingship and agreement or harmony would have suited political discussions. The official home of the senate, The Curia (Senate House), an Etruscan building but updated in later centuries, saw gatherings of up to a thousand senates and magistrates, and was gifted a statue of the winged goddess Victory, by Augustus, which stood on the dais watching over all proceedings. As noted already many political leaders also held religious offices and in fact it was expected and would afford politicians further respect as well as creating a persona of dignity and integrity.

A role that both bridged religion and politics was that of Censor. Censors were elected every five years, and it was a political role that included conducting a census of the city and issuing public contracts for construction. However, there was also a religious facet in that they performed an important ritual purification of the city as part of their duties. The role of the emperor was also both religious and political and from Emperor Augustus onwards the emperor was regarded as both a leader and, in the imitation of God Mars, he was the pater familias, father of Rome, expected to guide, inspire and set example by his life and deeds. He must be beyond reproach and Augustus displayed this most clearly in the exile of his daughter Julia, when her moral behaviour was called into question.

In the military triumphs as well, it was known that on occasion the face of the leader, riding in his chariot (often the military leader or the emperor) was reddened with cinnabar so that they looked like the terracotta image of Jupiter.

Spells, Magic and Superstition.

Ancient Rome had its fair share of sceptics and also those whom believed in magic and were willing to use spells and superstitions. The Emperor Septimus Severus was well known to have been very interested in superstitions and the mysterious, especially those that were exotically eastern! Yet Columella writes in his agricultural handbook:

> He (the estate manager) must not let fortune-tellers or sorceresses on to the farm; both these types of silly superstition make unsophisticated people spend money, and lead to wrongdoing.
> Columella, De Re Rustica, 1.8.6

Plutarch in *The Rise of Rome* also advises against superstition, comparing the childish insolence of King Tullus in giving himself over to superstitions, to the seemly piety of Numa. Plutarch shares that it was deemed to be a fulfilment of his own superstition that Tullus was killed by being struck by lightning. Some superstitions may also have been born from wishful thinking. For example, the Romans decorated their banqueting tables with violets in the belief that they would provide a charm against drunkenness, while wearing a violet the next day would help relieve a hangover.

The works of Virgil, Apuleius, Lucan and Horace also all feature references to magical experiences, witches, witchcraft and love charms. Horace's fifth Epode describes the creation of a love potion by four witches. In his work 1st century CE work *Pharsalia* the writer Lucan talks about the witch Erichto with a negative perspective and puts forward the viewpoint that witchcraft was a dark power that causes destruction. Ovid in *Fasti* describes a spell or ritual to remove ghosts from the household that involved placing nine black beans in the mouth and then proceeding to spit them out while walking around the house, the ghost would follow and pick them up. Once finished you would wash your hands and tell the ghost/s 'Good spirits, go now!' and hopefully the ghost would oblige! This was to performed three times for best effectiveness and ideally in the month of May.

Devotio may also has been used as part of rituals or spells. Devotio was a name given to a magical charm which took the form of a wax image of a person. This wax image was handled in a way that it was hoped would achieve a similar outcome with the person it depicted, such as to make the person feel pain or in the hopes they felt love. It was considered a sacrificial item in place of the person it depicted. For example, it could be melted and this it was hoped would result in the person also melting with/in love with the owner. There has also been much evidence found at Roman bathhouses of apotropaic symbols and devices, such as amulets, that would ward off magic, water daemons and the evil envious eye that one was exposed to when naked and vulnerable.

As for superstitions many considered it bad luck to marry in May, as the month held the festival of Lemures. Other superstitions included not wearing your toga while lying on your bed alive (many citizens only wore their best toga on their bed on the day of their funeral), greeting summer lightning with the clapping of hands and never sweeping the floor or table clean while a person is rising to leave. When commenting on superstitions Pliny the Elder says that:

these usages have been established by person who entertained a belief that the gods are ever present, in all our affairs, and at all hours
Pliny, *Natural Histories*, Book 28. Chapter 5. Line 56

Charms, amulets (such as that of the *mano fica* gesture) and incantations were also used as part of medicine and healing procedures and would accompany herbal, and plant remedies, as well as being used on their own. In one of his books, Marcus Terentisu Varro shares a traditional and 'rustic' charm he has heard of to cure painful feet:

> *I have heard Tarquenna say that when a man's feet begin to hurt he may be cured if he will think of you: 'I am thinking of you, cure my feet. The pain go in the ground, and may my feet be sound.' He bids you chant this thrice nine times, touch the ground, spit on it, and be fasting while you chant.*
>
> Varro, *On Agriculture*, Book 1, 24-25

The power of three was utilised in many such Roman incantations. The Goddess Carna (of the hinges) also uses the power of three in her healing of a wounded child:

> *Three times in a row she touches the doorposts with a branch of arbutus, three times with a branch of arbutus she marks the threshold...*
>
> Ovid, *Fasti*, Book 6, lines 155 – 157.

It is also not surprising in a culture and people that so valued and practiced the art of rhetoric, that they would firmly believe in the power of words. Pliny the Elder shares about incantations in *Natural History*:

> *...as individuals, all our wisest men reject belief in them, although, as a body, the public at all times believe in them unconsciously. In fact, the sacrifice of victims without a prayer is supposed to be of no effect; without it too the gods are not thought to be properly consulted."*
>
> Pliny *Natural History*, 28. iii

Words could also therefore act as an important point of communion and communication with the divine. It was also important to heal the genius or soul along with the body and incantations, charms and words were seen as suitable and affective treatment for this aspect of self. Pliny goes on to stress that effectiveness was also insured by precise and correct words, with no interruptions and *"not a single word may be omitted or pronounced out of its place."* (*Natural History*, 28. Iii). He gives an example of a man struck by lightning whom had omitted certain words in an address to Jupiter.

The Romans also believed in signs or portents in nature. Tacitus writes of:

> ...*portents in the sky and on the earth, thunderbolts and other premonitions of good and evil, some doubtful, some obvious.*
> Tacitus, *The Histories*, Book 1.3

He shares a belief that current portents, such as earthquakes, fires and volcanic eruptions foretold and then amplified the horrors of civil strife during the time of the four emperors. The destruction of the Capitol Temple of Jupiter in the great fire of 69 CE was also seen by many as a portent of the decline of Rome.

Invidia was the roman goddess of envy, revenge and the evil eye. Ovid describes her as having a poisoned tongue and the Vestal virgins were noted to have placed symbolic charms under the chariot of a Roman general to ward against her gaze.

Tacitus also mentions in *Annals* the case of a young widow, daughter of Barea Soranus, who was accused of spending large amounts of money on magic. Her plea to innocence was that she has never used black magic, magicians or invoked the forbidden gods. Such forbidden gods and magic included particular Egyptian deities and Jewish rites. Emperor Tiberius went so far as to outlaw both, though Isis remained popular in Rome despite a well-known connection to magic. Necromancy was also viewed with hostility in ancient Rome, yet it was sometimes considered a part of oracular practices despite great disapproval.

Chapter 6

Sacred Time

The gods' temples and ears are open, no tongue conceives
prayers that fall useless, and things that are said carry
weight.
Words of the God Janus, in Ovid's *Fasti*, Book 1.
Lines 181-182

Festivals and rituals were an important part of both family and social life, and the Roman state religion and deity worship. Rites and rituals were practised with vigilance and discipline and were believed to be integral not just to keeping the favour of the gods and ancestors but also to retain the equilibrium of existence. Religious ceremonies also underlined the role of the gods in Rome's destiny and greatness. Let us explore some ways in which the Ancient Romans marked and celebrated sacred time.

Games and Pastimes

On pantomime "It sharpens the wits, it exercises the body, it
delights the spectator, it instructs him in the history of bygone
days ... while eye and ear are held beneath the spell of flute
and cymbal and of graceful dance ... you will find the evil-doer
greeted with curses and his victim with sympathetic tears."
Lucian, Satirist of the 2nd century CE

By the 1st century CE there were about one hundred and fifty-nine Roman holy-days, with ninety-three of these devoted to public games, such as chariot races and gladiatorial combat. Originally most of these performances were organised for religious reasons; plays and chariot races were to honour the gods and at the funerals of great men you would find gladiator fights. Often the large entertainments would begin with a procession that would lead the public to the Circus Maximus or colosseum and in this procession would be carried the figures of gods carried on litters, accompanied by dancers, musicians and other entertainers. There were games which were held simply to entertain the people, often being sponsored by the emperor or rich patrons to ensure popularity and keep the masses happy or distracted. In these games religious iconography and symbology was often still included, but was not the primary focus or objective.

The principal games of the year were the Ludi Romani, held in honour of Jupiter and were established early on in the history of Rome. Eventually they were held annually mid- September from the 4th to the 19th September (thought the dates vary and change throughout the history of Rome). These dates often coincided with the return of the Roman Army who would frequently go out on campaign during the summer and their triumphal procession through the city formed part of the games. The festival would involve the hugely popular chariot races, where the Roman people could follow their favourite team, the blues, the greens, the whites or the reds, as well as smaller competitions between fighters and displays of dance, music and horsemanship. There were significant games dedicated to other deities also, such as the games of Flora which were founded in 241 -238 BCE.

Plays and theatre were considered holy to Bacchus, the Roman God of Wine, drama and festivities. Theatre productions, plays and recitals of poetry were also dedicated to the Goddess Venus. Many plays also featured gods, goddesses and heroes, such as Plautus' play Amphitruo, which features Jupiter and Mercury as the main characters and Apuleius' famous 'The Golden Ass' in which the Goddess Isis is a central character.

Gods and Goddesses also featured in literature and poetry, such as Venus, in the poems of Catullus, whom he devoted much of his work to and Ovid made invocations to Apollo in his work. Apollo and Minerva were connected to music, both the learning, playing and performance of. Romans also enjoyed Pantomime, in which actors portrayed the gods through the use of masks, costume, specific gestures and movements.

The favourite pastime of gambling was connected to the God Mercury and the Goddess Fortuna and they were invoked by the lucky and unlucky. Horse racing has a particular connection to the agricultural God Mars and his horse racing was often included in his iconography, worship and festivals. Goddess Nemesis was the patron goddess of gladiatorial games and some amphitheatres had a shrine to her, known as a Nemeseum.

Festivals and Holy Days

The populace longs for two things: bread and circus games
Juvenal

Throughout the calendar year the Romans had numerous public holidays that often coincided with a feast day or festival. The veneration of ancient gods and goddesses was chiefly connected with the seasons, with deities thematic to particular activities and produce relevant to periods of time within the cycle of seed to harvest. For the ancient Romans, calendars were a device for regulating and organising social and religious affairs in connection to these seasonal cycles. It was ancient Roman belief that their calendar was devised by the second King of Rome, Numa Pompilius (8th – 7th century BCE) and that it was his festival calendar that formed the foundations of political and religious life. By tradition it was then developed during the following centuries of the regal period.

It is believed that the Roman and Etruscan year was originally lunar, with each month being marked by the cycle of the moon from new to dark and then progressed to solar during the time of the Republic. We can credit the Romans with the twelve months of the year as we know them, which retain the length, sequence and names assigned to them during the times of Julius Caeser and Emperor Augustus. The official calendar of the year was drawn up by the pontiffs of these periods. Many of the months were named for deities, such as March for Mars, June for Juno and August for the Divine Emperor Augustus. The month was divided by holy days; *Calends* (the first of the month), the *Nones* (the fifth or seventh day) and the *Ides* (the thirteenth or fifteenth). Many of the calends and Ides were dedicated to the gods. For example, eight ides were dedicated to Jupiter, calends in general were sacred to Juno and the calends of March was dedicated to Mars. Also, on the Ides of each month a sheep was sacrificed on the Capitoline to Jupiter.

The Romans also gave us a day starting at night in contrast to the Greek day starting at sunset, or, at sunrise with the Babylonians. The passage of the sun was followed and the peak of the sun, and so midday, was announced every day by a member of the consul in the Forum to the general populace. And so, two halves of the day were marked, formed and honoured.

Their weekdays in both name and energy were connected to the seven known planets and the associated seven deities:

Monday – *Dies Lunae* – Goddess Luna, Goddess of the moon

Tuesday – *Dies Martis* – God Mars, God of agriculture and father of Rome

Wednesday – *Dies Mercurii* – God Mercury, God of commerce and trade

Thursday – *Dies Jovis* – God Jupiter, King of the sky and thunder

Friday – *Dies Veneris* – Goddess Venus, Goddess of vegetation, beauty and fertility
Saturday – *Dies Saturni* – God Saturn, Father of time and abundance
Sunday – *Dies Solis* – God Sol, God of the Sun

For your own practice, you may want to connect to or honour (by lighting incense or saying a prayer) the relevant deity on their holy day.

The majority of the Roman year was made up of *dies fasti*, good days. These days were those that one could conduct judicial and civil business without running the risk of offending the gods. There were also *dies nefasti* that ranged from 176 days to 135 days of the year, depending on the century. These days were the days on which the Romans celebrated their religious rites and festivals. These days were no-business days when no public assemblies or official judgements could be held. Some of these *dies nefasti* were public holidays and others, called *ludi,* were set aside for the public games. There was also fourteen days of the year when business might be conducted but only after rites and ceremonies were performed in the first half of the day. There was variance in these number of days in different reigns of Emperors, Marcus Aurelius, for example, restored the business year to 230 days.

A significant day in the year was the Feast of Fortuna. All the luck that happened on that day, good or bad, was supposed to be an omen of the entire year to come! Such days can be found noted in the Calendar of Philocalus (354 CE) and the Calendar of Antium (1st Century BCE), as well as in the memoirs, gravestones and dedication words of many monuments and temples. Most festivals and holy days are also noted in *Fasti*, Roman calendars such as the above which marked important religious days and official events. They were most frequently found as carved inscriptions or manuscripts that were placed in prominent public areas. They were originally compiled and used by priests and officials. The first Fasti to be made public was made so by the aedile (a type of magistrate) Gnaeus Flavius in the Forum in 304 BCE. Later on, this spot, to mark the significance of the action, was placed the Shrine of Concordia, the goddess who personified harmony and concord (agreement and unity) and ruled over the order of the state. The *fasti antiates maiores* is the earliest surviving fasti that we have as a resource. Others examples include the *Fasti Ostienses* from the port of Ostia, the principal seaport of Rome. This fasti like others was placed at the temple of Vulcan, the patron god of Ostia. Another is the fasti that was erected in the temple of Hercules of the Muses by the Roman senator Fulvius Flaccus. It lists notices of important dates, such as temple dedications and military victories by Roman generals. Also left to us is Ovid's text, *Fasti*, a work of literature that is a mix of religious calendar, mythology and commentary.

Almost all festivals had some association with fertility, agriculture and the cycles of the seasonal year but some were also in commemoration of particular events, such as battles and the dedication of temples. Emperor Trajan hosted games that latest over one hundred days to mark his victory over the Dacians. Some festivals were older than Rome itself and inherited from Etruscan traditions. Public festivals and sacred days could be marked by chariot races, gladiatorial games, processions, public sacrifice and celebrated through banquets or comedies and plays, such as those written by Plautus and Terence.

Games were given in honour of the gods, to appease and to worship. There was also the idea that the games reflected the splendour and strength of the gods onto the patrons, combatants, actors and racers and sometimes even endowed them with the incarnation of the deities. There were games throughout the year that were dedicated to Jupiter, Mars, Apollo, Ceres, Cybele and Flora. Certain deities were also particularly linked with a particular type of games. Circus games (chariot racing) for example, were part of the religious calendar. These games, were both religious and social. Consus, an ancient Italian deity of grain storage had an altar at the end of Circus Maximus racetrack. This altar was covered and only uncovered during the games there. It was believed that Romulus established the earliest races to honour Consus. At the circus was also a statue to Pollentia, the Goddess of Might, who was thought to favour competitive games and bestow her favour on competitors, as well as shrines to Sol and Luna at the centre of the arena which were flanked by Egyptian obelisks set up in honour of the sun. The whole site of the Circus maximus itself also had religious origins as the place of worship for the cult of the deities Murcia, Consus and Sol. The turning posts of the Circus at either end of the spina were adorned with seven eggs sacred to the demi-gods Castor and Pollux and Neptune's dolphins were used as the seven lap counters for the races. Horse racing in general had a particular connection to the God Mars. There was even religious symbolism in the gladiatorial shows of Flavian amphitheatre. An attendant dressed as the Etruscan god of the dead, Charun or the God Mercury, would be the one to enter the arena, assess the state of a fallen gladiatorial with a mallet to the head and then accompany its removal.

A Year of Festivals

March was traditionally the first month of the year and marked the beginning of the military and farming season. It was honoured for these reasons even when the first month of the calendar became January. March was the sacred month of Mars, named for him, in honour of him at the divine father of Rome. Festivals and celebrations in his honour as an agricultural God marked the rebirth of the agricultural year in this month. Ovid claims that it was actually Latium that had March as the first month of the year and Romulus himself who named the month for his father. In *Fasti*, Ovid shares that the Sabines had March as their fourth month of the year, their year beginning around the rebirth of the winter sun. The following month of April was deemed to be Venus' in honour of her as the origin of the race of Romans (as the mother of Aeneas). Ovid argues that it was King Numa that added two months to the beginning of the year, before March, one to honour the God Janus (January) and another for the ancestors (February) and ruled that the Romans must use those months for the celebration and remembrance of those beings.

Here are some of the primary festivals of the Roman calendar (there are so many that I have been very select!). We begin with March, for the old calendar of the ancient Romans and the first month of the agricultural year.

March

1st March The traditional birth day of Mars and a day to honour and worship him.

1st March Matronalia. Worship of Juno Lucina, the Goddess of childbirth and bringing children into the light. Honoured Juno as the Goddess of Motherhood and prayers and offerings were said to Juno and Mars (her son). Husbands also gave gifts to their wives on this day and women to their female slaves.

19th – 23rd March Quinquatrus meaning the 'five days joined'. Festival of Minerva. The 19th March was to be kept free from all blood-shedding of any kind as this was believed to be the birth day of Minerva. Following this circus and gladiatorial games were held in her honour on the 20th and 21st. The 23rd of March was held sacred to the 'valiant' Mars.

17th March Luberalia A model of a giant phallus was pulled around the countryside on a cart as part of fertility rites and celebrations to begin the agricultural year.

April

4th April Megalesia. Spring Festival for the Great Mother Cybele and her son Attis. Procession of her priests and worshippers through Rome with, what was described as, wild and erratic music, singing and dancing by her priests. Games and theatre were also enjoyed by everyone.

12th – 19th April Ludi Ceriales or the Cerialia. The Festival of Ceres, consecrated in 202 BCE. On the festival high day of 15th April, a pregnant cow was sacrificed. Ritual and ceremony throughout this festival for a fertile and abundant agricultural year.

21st April Traditional Founding Day of Rome by Romulus, on the feast of Pales (Parilia / *Palilia*.), named for the god of Shepherds. It was a purification feast to the ancient pastoral God Pales. It remembered the contest between Romulus and Remus and Remus's fateful leaping over the boundaries. This date was later changed to the Festival of Natalis Urbis by Emperor Hadrian and celebrated across the Empire.

May

28th April – 3 May Floralia or Ludi Florales, Festival of the Goddess Flora, Goddess of flowers and spring. Games were held in her honour to ensure the blossoming of all flowers in spring. Garlands of flowers were placed on her statues and festival participants. For the month of May the armies' standards were decked with flowers in her honour.

9th May Lumeria A festival to appease the undead. The 9th, 11th and 13th of May were used for rituals of the dead as at this time it was believed that the Lemures (evil spirits or ghosts) would haunt houses. Rituals involved mostly ceremonies to appease the dead, such as offerings taken to graves and rites performed by the Pater Familias inside the house itself to appease family *Manes* (souls of dead ancestors). The temples were shut on these days and no marriages were conducted.

Around 29th May/ end of May Ambarvalia. Festival involving the rite of purification of land. It was participated in by farmers and all agricultural work stopped for festival activities. A procession took place on the land around Rome in which evil would be driven away from the crops and rituals undertaken to purify the crops to ensure their continued growth. The festival involved the worship of Mars, Liber, Ceres and Janus.

June

9th June Vestalia An ancient festival that pre-dated Rome and connected to the purification of the fields and home. It may have been Latin in origin. On the days before and after the Vestalia the vestal virgins cleaned and purified the Temple of Vesta, no public business was allowed to be conducted in Rome. Similar was conducted in the home and the hearths of temples and home cleaned and restored.

11th June Matralia A festival of Mothers, connected to the Goddess Mater Matuta, the Goddess of growth and childbirth. The festival was connected with birth and the care of children and women. The temple of Mater Matuta was decorated with flowers by newly married women.

25th – 26th June The Ludi Taurei Quinquennales were games to honour the gods of the underworld. They were held every five years and were held in hopes to ward off pestilence and plague.

July

5th July The Poplifugia. The Day that Romulus disappeared, or alternatively ascended to heaven and became a God. Originally July was named for the divine form that he took when he became a God but was later named in honour of Julius Ceaser.

6th to 13th July The Games of Apollo, in which he was celebrated as a sun-God in the hope that he would ripen the crops for harvest.

25th July Furrinalia A festival in honour of the Goddess Furrina, an Etruscan Goddess of Springs and water. This Etruscan festival was older than the republic and her rites were conducted by her Flamen in the sacred grove on the Janiculum Hill. She was believed to be able to prevent drought.

August

19th August Vinalia Rustica was an agricultural festival involving ceremonies and rituals to protect the vines. The Flamen Dialis, who served the cult of Jupiter broke some of the first grapes off the vine as one of these rituals. The festival was also associated with Venus, as Goddess of vegetation and fertility.

23rd August Volcanalia The festival of Vulcan, the Roman god of primaeval fire and his aspect as the destructive power of volcanoes. His consorts, Maia and Hora, were also included in the celebrations, as were The Nymphs. The Mother of the Gods, Goddess Ops also played a part of the festival rites. This time marked the vine harvest. The volcanic rock of the area was known and celebrated to bring fertility in particular to the vines and Vulcan was honoured for this.

28th August The festival games (Ludi circenses) of Luna and Sol. Chariot races were held at the Circus Maximus, and other associated events such as amphitheatre entertainments, in honour of the deities Sol and Luna.

September
4th to 19th September Ludi Romani, Games in Honour of Jupiter Optimus Maximus and the most important games of the year. They had their origin in a triumph but became the most important games of the year. The games involved a procession from the capitol to the circus maximus. There was also chariot racing and sacrifices to Jupiter.

13th September Feast Day of Jupiter and the day of dedication for the Temple of Jupiter.

13th September The Lectisternium Feast in honour of the Capitoline Triad, in which the three principal deities, Jupiter, Juno and Minerva were honoured with a great banquet.

October
14th October Festival of the Penates. The Di Penates were the gods of the store cupboards and were honoured in the home on this festival. Garlands of flowers were placed upon the household shrines and small offerings such as fruit or salt were offered on the shrine or thrown into the hearth fire and accompanied by prayers to beseech the Penates to continue looking after the house and the household.

15th October The Capitoline Games that were held in honour of Jupiter. These games were organised by the priests of Jupiter

Capitoline. The games were believed to have been older the Roman republic or possibly were held in remembrance of the conquest of the Etruscan city of Veii. There were also sacrifices made to Mars on this day to ensure good crops, including the sacrifice of a significant horse from the chariot races of this day.

19th October Armilustrium. The festival marking the end of the military season and was a festival in honour of Mars. Celebrated on the open square on the Aventine Hill where were the graves of Remus and Titus Tatius.

November

November 4th to 17th The Ludi Plebeii. The Plebeian Games were held in honour of Jupiter and involved chariot racing in the circus maximus. It was organised by the plebeian aediles. They were the second most important games in the yearly calendar, second only to the Ludi Romani.

December

17th December (In the Republic it was extended to several days following) Saturnalia One of the most popular of Roman festivals, it was a Celebration of the God Saturn and a festival of renewal. It was a time of family gatherings, gift exchanging, well wishes and making way for the birth of the new. Part of the celebrations was a role reversal of masters waiting on their slaves. Gambling and betting were forbidden at this time.

19th December A festival to honour Ops, the consort of Saturn and Goddess of grain and agricultural resources. This festival and rites were concerned with the right storing of grain and at this time the sowing of crops was finished.

25th December Feast of Sol, the Sun God, celebrating the return or rebirth of the sun.

January

1st January Feast Day of Janus. The first of January was dedicated to the God Janus. A day, for like the double headed Janus, looking back at the old year and forward to the new year. Presents were exchanged, in particular oils lamps, which were symbolic of lighting the path of the new year. It was important to exchange good wishes on this day.

11th and 15th January Carmentalia for the Goddess Carmenta, Goddess of prophecy and birth. Her festival of threshold was chiefly observed by women and may have included a birth focus or theme (the month for marriage, April, was 9 months earlier).

February

15th February Lupercalia, festival of fertility, farming and foundation. A very popular festival, associated with deities such as Goddess Luperca, She-Wolf of Rome, God Faustus and the deified Romulus. Involved the running of noble sons in a circular route around the base of Palatine Hill, following the boundaries of Romulus' original settlement.

13th February to 21st February Paternalia and the Feralia, festivals of remembrance, family and a time to honour the ancestors, Lares and Manes. Traditionally celebrated with visits to tombs, making of offerings to ancestors and ceremonial meals and banquets eaten at the tombs. Feralia comes from the Latin *ferre*, meaning 'to bring'. Parentalia refers to honouring the dead.

Rites of Passage

The life given us, by nature is short; but the memory of a well-spent life is eternal.
Cicero

Pregnancy, Birth and Coming of Age

There were many protectors and deities for a woman that was going through pregnancy and for the baby itself. The household Lares would, of course, preside over the whole process, the Goddess Alemona was guardian of foetus's and Partula was the goddess of delivery. Decima was the Roman goddess who presided over the ninth month of pregnancy and was considered one of the fates. A candle was also lit for Goddess Candelifera, the goddess who supported women in childbirth. A genius appeared at the birth of an infant to form its personality and the Goddess Vagitanus was she of the first life-affirming cry of the baby. Following birth, the Goddess Cunina could be requested to watch over the cradle and Rumina, was the Goddess of breastfeeding. Often breastmilk would be offered in her honour or milk given as a libation to request her assistance with milk flow. The Goddess Juno Lucinda, and her son Mars, were also both deities that governed conception and childbirth, as Juno conceived Mars through union with a flower. During labour it was advised that a woman pray to these gods for support and loosen (or unbind) her hair and this release would bring ease to the delivery. An offering of flowers to the gods would also support the mother in this. The flowers of cherry or plum blossom were considered appropriate offerings. It was the goddess Abeona who presided over the first steps of a child and then guided the steps of the child back to its home.

In ancient Rome there was a high mortality rate at birth and in childhood and a third of children did not make it to their first birthday. However, babies were still loved and valued, as evidenced by the high number of children tombstones and dedications that can be found. Perhaps this mortality rate influenced some of the post-birth practices of the ancient Romans. At nine days old a boy child was given a charm amulet (or talisman) of protection, called *bulla*, at eight days for a girl.

Many of these *bullae* have been found with the image of the she-wolf, Lupa, upon them[12]. This day was called the *dies lustricus* (day of purification) and would be celebrated by friends and family, who would bring gifts. The *bulla* would later be given to the household Lares when the boy came of age, or the girl married.

The children were also named at this time of eight or nine days old. Boys were given three names, a *praenomen*, his own name, then the *nomen* of his gens (a tribe of people who claimed descent a common ancestor) and also the *cogonomen* of his family. Examples are the politician Marcus Tullius Cicero and Marcus Plautius Silvanus (his name, his clan's name and then his family/specific branch from the wider clan). The first name was only used by intimates and men were more commonly addressed by their clan and family names, such as in the case of Gaius Julius Ceaser and this naming was an important element in the practice of *pietas*. Girls would often be given a feminized version of their father's, or a male relative's name such as Julius Ceaser's daughter was called Julia Caesaris and the famous courtesan Clodia and her brother Clodius. However, it is known for names to also be linked to the deities, such as the female name Fortunata, in honour of the Goddess Fortuna, as in the case of Julia Fortunata and Martia, meaning she who is devout to the God Mars. At this time of naming, prayers were also said and offerings made, for the health and happiness of the child. The child was only named if it were accepted by its father into the family. This acceptance would have been previously demonstrated in a ritual in which the father would pick the child up from the ground at his feet, where it has been placed. If a child was accepted, a wreath was hung upon the household doorposts to announce its arrival. Olive, celery and myrtle wreaths were common.

A boy would come of age around the age of sixteen, upon which they were released from their father's authority. This coming-of-age ceremony was marked by the boy removing his *bulla* and from then on, he would wear the plain white toga worn by Roman citizens. Goddess Juventas was the goddess of young men 'new to wearing the toga' (*dea novorum togatorum*) and especially guarded all those whom had just come of age. A young man's first trip to the barbers for a shave was also made a religious ceremony: the *depositio barbae*. Much festivity would be made of this coming of age with feasts where family and friends were welcome and the first cut was given to a chosen deity. The dates the emperors had their first shave were even recorded, such as Augustus in September 39 BCE. Nero consecrated the hairs of his first beard by placing them in a golden basket and made of offering of them to Jupiter Optimus Maximus on the Capitoline. One of the characters in the novel of Petronius in the same way offered his first beard hairs into a sacred box placed between the statues of Venus and his Lares in his private household shrine.

Marriage

Marriage in ancient Rome was a legal matter not solely religious, with laws governing both marriage, divorce, dowries and inheritance. Despite this, marriage was woven in ceremony, rites and rituals that were steeped in tradition and had religious symbology and connotations. One such tradition was that at twelve years old girls began to prepare for marriage, though she was often betrothed earlier. For boys it was generally agreed that they were ready from the age of fourteen. Many Romans also seem to have experienced several marriages throughout their lifetimes. Therefore, the ancient Romans may have experienced several times the many rites and rituals that mark this threshold and time of transition. The extent of some observations, however, seemingly varied depending on the class of family and their background of occupation and district. In general June was a popular month for weddings, being sacred to the Goddess of marriage, Juno, as long as the marriage was held after the 15ᵗʰ June, before then was ill-omened. Ovid shares that May was considered a very unlucky month to marry, as was March. It was also inauspicious to marry on the kalends, nones or ides of the month. April was considered the most auspicious month, being connected to the fertile vegetation spirit, Venus.

Juno was the Goddess who presided over marriage in general, both the initial ceremony, marital contracts and marital life. Cinxia was another Roman deity of marriage whose role was to protect the bride's girdle and Goddess Manturna would preside over the preservation of marriage. Sometimes sacrifices were also made to Ceres or Tellus Mater in rural weddings.

In *Annals*, Tacitus shares about the marriage of the Empress Messalina, third wife of Claudius, to her lover Senator Sillius in 48 CE. The marriage may not have happened, or have been mock performance part of a ritual or feast, however, the commentary gives us a glimpse at the attitudes towards marriage and some of the basic components:

Here is the consul designate, marrying the wife of the emperor, on a duly appointed day, in the presence of witnesses: here is the Empress, hearing the auspices, taking the bridal veil, sacrificing to the gods. Together they take their place at the wedding feast among their guests; there is an exchange of kisses and embraces, the night is passed in the delights of an honourable marriage.
Tacitus, *Annals*, 11, 32-37

It seems that the traditions remained the same throughout ancient Roman history, and for almost all levels of society. The day before her wedding day the bride-to-be would make an offering to the *Lares* of her family's household. The household was decorated with wreaths of symbolic flowers, such as marjoram, African lily, myrtle, rosemary and laurel branches. In the continuation of Latin tradition, the bride's wedding veil, the *flammeum* would often be red or orange and her tunic saffron yellow to signify the flame of the Goddess Vesta, the goddess of home and hearth. On top of her veil was placed a wreath made of verbena and marjoram, or myrtle and orange blossoms. The wedding day would begin at dawn at which time a sacrifice was made and perhaps a reading of entrails to check for signs, hopefully positive ones! They would exchange vows next and a wheat cake would be blessed by the priest. Then, in remembrance of capture of the Sabine women, the bride would 'flee' to her mother, but then be whisked away by her husband, who would then take her to his home. In another reference to the abduction of the Sabine women by Romulus, during the ceremony a bride's hair would be parted by the point of a spear (the Latin for spear gave Romulus his deified name Quirinius).

In the wedding procession to her new home, two maidens would carry the bride's distaff and her spindle and the bride would herself sometimes carry a torch, possibly made of twisted hawthorn twigs or pinewood. It was lit from the hearth and so contained the spirit of Vesta. This torch would then be thrown away when she reached her husband's house and whoever caught it was assured a long life. Other traditions included the carrying of nuts, sometimes within a rattle during the procession and these nuts would be thrown from the threshold of home and bless all those that caught them with fertility. Her husband would then lift her through the doorway, as it was bad luck for her feet to touch the threshold. Plutarch writes that the tradition of carrying the bride over the threshold was one that was believed by the Romans to stem all the way back to the time of Romulus, when the Sabine virgins were abducted and carried away to became the wives of the first Romans. In most households in Rome a bride having crossed the threshold to her new home would then straight away make an offering to the house's *Lar* and decorate its household shrine. Her new husband would offer her fire and water and them ceremoniously remove her headdress and girdle.

A tradition from Rome's rural farming districts is recorded by Pliny in which on the arrival of a bride to her new home she smeared the doorposts with wolf's fat and oil, and wound fillets of wool around it. The fat of the fearsome wolf was used as a charm against evil spirits. Only once she has performed this rite could she pass over the threshold and be received by her husband and be symbolically accepted as the materfamilias to her husband.[13]

The Goddess Fortuna was also known to protect and bless new brides and later on in marriage a useful ally may have been Viriplaca, a goddess who acted as a marriage guidance counsellor. Concord, Goddess of Harmony may also had been called on to bring harmony within marriage. Another deity was Hymen, the Greek God of Marriage whom the famous Roman poet Catullus wrote a poem to:

> *O Hymen, cover your brow with sweet-smelling marjoram, take the flame-coloured veil, come joyfully, wearing yellow shoes on your snow-white feet; excited by this happy day, sing the wedding-song in a ringing voice. Stamp on the ground and shake the pinewood torch.*
>
> Catullus, *Poems* 61 5-15

This poem is also similar to the bridal songs that were often sung to Roman household gods or chosen deity and it references some of the features of a typical roman marriage.

There was no religious taboo or ban on divorce, but if such an event was expected to happen then Goddess Juno may perhaps be called upon or made offering to, as she was the Goddess of Reconciliation.

Funerals

Sprinkle my ashes with pure wine and fragrant oil of spikenard:
Bring balsam, too, stranger, with crimson roses.
Tearless my urn enjoys unending spring.
I have not died, but changed my state.
Ausonius, *Epitaph*

As with the ideas of death and the afterlife, Roman funeral traditions and practices were sourced in those of the Etruscans. For them and so with early Romans, inhumation was more common than cremation. However, both were used and trends ebbed and flowed throughout the centuries and the choice was also sometimes dependant on the wealth and status of a family or person.

After death a Roman would be placed in honour in the family home with wreaths and torches surrounding their washed and clothed body and incense burnt. The body would have its feet facing towards the house door and its eyelids closed. The women of the family would lament the death and the hearth fire was extinguished. The laying out of the body would occur for up to seven days, in which family and friends could pay their last respects and the name of the dead person was spoken out loud intermittently. There may also be *praeficae*, hired female mourners.

The funeral procession of an open coffin would be accompanied by torch bearers and sometimes official mourners. If it could be afforded official mourners may also have been used to honour the ancestors of the deceased, being dressed in ancestor's clothes, wearing masks depicting the dead or riding in chariots. Other times family members played this role.

Pliny the Elder shares that:

Wax portraits were made as images to accompany the family's funeral processions. So, whenever someone died, every member of the family who had ever existed was present.
Pliny, *Natural History*, 35, 2

However, these wax death masks were actually made when the person was alive, mostly relatively young, around thirty-five to forty years old. They often accompanied an aristocrat reaching a certain rank, much like getting a portrait painted when you get the big promotion at work. They were then, truly the faces and features of the person of whom they depicted and were only called death masks due to their being worn during their descendants' funerals. They also emphasise the importance that the Romans placed on the portrait and the central depiction of the sacred head and face (location of the soul) in both the art and sculpture, memorial and dedication. After the funeral the masks would be placed back near the house shrine, often accompanying a gallery of family masks, where the ancestors were honoured. The masks would be brought out again for the next funeral. By the end of the republic portrait busts were beginning to overtake masks in popularity.

Roman inhumations or cremations, both of which were accepted, always took place outside of the city and burials of the body, or the cremation urns, normally lined the out-going streets. It was illegal to bury the dead within the sacred sanctum of Rome, except for children under ten days old. Cemeteries were also used outside of the city walls. If cremation was chosen it often took place on a pyre near the site of burial.

Some early Etruscan burials in the areas surrounding Rome were well-style burials, rock cut tombs, and cave like tombs carved from cliffs and hills or underground circular chambre tombs with burial mounds on top. In the Roman period there were also above ground rectangular shaped tombs and the variations are much down to family preference and social trends.

In the earliest burials of Rome found beneath the forum there is both inhumation and cremation urns. These Etruscan-style cremation urns were circular in nature, often in the shape of, and styled as a hut, reflecting the homes of the earliest Roman residents. These were set in small, circular, deep pits. Later urns and chests became more popular for housing the ashes and grave goods. The Romans continued these styles and sometimes even reused tombs, adding Roman columns and porticos.

Emperors were often buried in their large mausoleums and those with wealth in family tombs, often with associated funerary gardens or groves. Almost all could afford at least to have their graves or burial urns topped by a decorated or inscribed amphora buried into the ground to mark the grave site. The wealthier used marble for their dedication and epithet plaques. Food, favourite items and jewellery were common items to be buried with the dead and shoes have also been found. The exception to this was that gold could not be buried with the dead, as per the customs recorded in the ancient Twelve Tablets. The very poor, however, were sometimes buried at night without ceremony or had just wooden grave markers. Coffins ranged from a sack to a stone coffin depending on your wealth and embalming was chosen by some but not believed as necessary. Many Romans chose to join burial clubs which were centred around a temple and deity and the club would ensure your proper burial after death.

In all cases the person would be buried underground or in a tomb so that the body was out of sight from the heavenly gods. It was now in the care or hands of the underworld gods and this out of sight, out of mind approach severed the relationship between the upperworld gods and the deceased human and avoided causing offence to the upperworld gods. On a practical level burial also avoided religious pollution as well as easing the passage of the dead soul to the underworld, so it was not left roaming in the upper worlds.

In most levels of Roman society, it was common to depict mythology, battle scenes and creatures upon burial art, sometimes with religious connotations. From elaborately decorated Etruscan tombs, to Roman sarcophagi and mausoleums, decoration could be found in all, that affirmed the beliefs of life and death. This decoration, as well as furnishings and grave goods, were used much in the same way as for they were for living; to adorn the home of the person interned. It was important to have a fitting *domus aeterna*, eternal home. Decoration often included nature, such as trees, flowers, countryside scenes and gardens, household items, rooms and activities, as well as scenes with dolphins, birds, feasts, cupids or in the case of children, favourite toys. Within the tombs, urns and sarcophagi was placed leaves of the evergreen plant box, a symbol of everlasting life. Bay leaves and laurels were placed on or around the heads of the deceased. Offerings of food have also been found in burial sites and funeral pyres. Candles were also placed in tombs for illumination in death's darkness. Shoes were also a common inclusion in burial, for travelling to the underworld. The same was the case for coins that were thought to be given to Mercury, Tellus Mater or other underworld deities to ensure safe and easeful passage.

It was common for a banquet to follow any funerary rite and sometimes if the person was deemed important enough a funeral oration would be given. The family were also expected to return to the chosen burial site, especially during the official mourning period. They were first to return eight days following the burial to conduct a sort of family picnic, with food and drink for the living and a proportional offering to the dead. Furniture such as couches and chairs were placed inside tombs for the departed souls to use during these feasts. Thereafter similar and regular visits were made, such as on the deceased birthdays and during Paternalia.

Roman soldiers who died in service were cremated and their ashes were placed inside a jar, pot or stone box and buried in the cemetery outside of his fort. If there was not a body available for burial or cremation a *cenotaphium* or 'dwelling place' could be made for the soul to reside in. It was called in by repeating the name of the person three times and was often decorated like a normal tomb or sarcophagus, with depictions of the person.

Part II

Chapter 7

Introduction to the Gods and Goddesses of Rome

The existence of the gods is a helpful thing; so, let us
believe in them.
Let us offer wine and incense on ancient altars.
The gods do not live in a state of quiet repose, like sleep.
Divine power is all around us: live a moral life!
Ovid

There were many hundreds of deities in ancient Rome. Many we only know by name and some we only know from a single occurrence of their name in an ancient text or dedication. A portion of these hundreds were known as single function deities or *numina*, meaning that they were solely present or invoked for a single function or instance. An example of this is the Goddess Abeona who was required a sacrifice as she watched over the first few steps of a child, after these first few steps there were other deities or guardians that would take over and this was her sole contribution. Many of the single function deities reflect the many concerns and anxieties that governed daily life in ancient Rome. When life is so fragile, fear could be very present and might necessitate the need for constant protection and support. It is believed that most major deities were a development of *Numina*, divine spirits or energies, that were originally spirits of a place such as a spring, cave, field or tree. Many of the original spirits or deities were non-gendered and personifications of place or idea, but gradually developed into, or acquired, personalities, names and mythologies. An example of this is Venus whose name is neither male or female, but encompasses all growing vegetation.

Some deities were so old that their function had already been forgotten by the time Roman historians became prolific with their writing in the 1st – 3rd centuries CE. Some deities were only known *because* they had a festival that was still celebrated. The Romans were also not averse to creating a new god for an occasion or a function; if one was needed, one was found. If the name of a deity had been forgotten, but the festival, rite or function remained, a new god sometimes was created to fit the job title.

We do know that many of the gods and goddesses of Rome have their roots in Etruscan, Sabine and Latin deities and mythology. These three roots of origin, Etruscan, Latin and Sabine, find their representation in the gods and goddesses included in the following chapters. I have shared, where I can, from which peoples each deity derives, though some do cross over and were recognised by name or similar form in all three cultures.

The religion of ancient Rome with its gods and goddesses and their associated rites and festivals began with the early farming families, and some were associated with very specific families, tribes or trades and crafts of the agricultural community. Sometimes these gods were abstract and were chiefly associated with natural phenomenon. It was also believed that in the earliest times the gods frequently visited the earth and sometimes lived among men. Janus and Saturn were believed to be rulers of the earliest time and peoples, a time when humans received the gods as their earthly kings. Saturn, ruled a golden age in Latium and Janus ruled in the area near Rome called Janiculum, where it was said justice and peace was upheld above all things. At the time of Janus, it was said that the land of Rome was an untouched forest in which he would pasture his cattle. It was Saturn, Janus and Vulcan that were considered the most ancient gods that ruled the lands and tribes surrounding Rome before the foundation of the city. It was believed the gods eventually left the earth, with Astraia, the Goddess of Justice being the last to depart as a result of the increasing lawlessness that came with the start of the bronze age. This time was the rise of Jupiter, who brought silver, bronze and iron to humans. The father of the Roman people was believed to be the God Mars, who shared a special relationship with his race.

Virgil, in the Aeneid shares about the age of iron, in which Jupiter was supreme of the gods, followed second in supremacy by Juno. This age of Jupiter had a new golden rule. The golden rule, as shared by Virgil, required that Jupiter was always invoked or prayed to first. Virgil warns of the breaking this rule in *Aeneid* when the Latins invoke Jupiter last and so lose the final battle. Ovid, however, shares in *Fasti* that it was Janus that still had the honour of always being invoked and honoured first in all prayers and invocations as he was the chaos itself that came before the existence of the gods and he reign opened the doorway to existence of humanity as we know it. By the time of the Republic, it was considered that the great gods or primary deities, were the Etruscan influenced Capitoline Triad, Jupiter, Juno and Minerva. Their temples could be found on Capitoline Hill.

The Capitoline Triad were three of five official and supreme gods of the Roman state; Jupiter, Juno, Minerva, Roma, the goddess of Rome and the guardian spirit (the genius) of the emperor. Only Mars and Janus were considered of equal important to any of these five. Additional to this, in just the city and region of Rome itself, were hundreds of gods, many of local cults and districts, some specific to certain trades, areas of land or locations such as the home, or springs, and others that were linked with rites of passage such as birth, death and coming of age.

There were also deities that were personifications of virtues; those virtues that were most important to the Romans and contributed to their way of being and doing. These were often deities that could be linked as epithets to other deities or emperors as well as worshipped themselves as a deity or as a concept. The principle four of these are Virtus, Victory, Discipulina, and Fortuna. Virtus or Virtue was often depicted with a helmet and with an amazon style tunic leaving one breast uncovered and had connections with the emperor, the state and the army. Victory or Victoria was also popular with the army and was depicted with wings, a palm branch and a wreath. She could be worshipped as Victory of the army, as an epithet for specific person such as the emperor, as the presiding goddess over a particular battle, or just as victory in general. Discipulina or disciplina, was a goddess connected with discipline and responsibility. She gave divine sanction to order and punishment that was enforced by the state and its figures of authority. Fortuna, or Fortune, was perhaps the most favoured and celebrated. She presided over fortune is all aspects of life, from luck in a card game, to avoiding an accident, to an abundance of crops and good weather. She was depicted as a goddess with a ship's rudder, globe and wheel.

Where an epithet was given to a deity it was considered an aspect of that deity, with that aspect often having its own separate temple, festival/celebration, rites and rituals for the thematic function they performed, such as Juno Fortuna and Venus Fortuna. An epithet could also be referenced by the inclusion of a symbol in a statue or depiction of the Goddess, for example, when the epithet or goddess Abundantia was linked to another goddess, reference to her may be made through a depiction or reference to coins or a full cornucopia.

Generally, in Roman religious iconography, in order to distinguish man from deities the gods were depicted as larger, barefoot, semi-nude or nude in order to display their perfection and often with a reference or depiction of some sort of aspect of nature. Humans were in contrast smaller in size and always fully clothed. The oldest gods were also frequently described as bearded, such as a reflective Janus *"stroking the beard that hung down to his chest"* (Ovid, *Fasti*, Book 1. Line 260). The beard was a symbol of their archaic age, just as the ancestors were often described also as the 'un-shaven' ones, in contrast to the clean-shaven Romans.

Other features set them apart such as the beaded woollen fillet (*infula*) worn by Juno that signified her imperial status. Similar to this a crescent shaped crown or *stephane* (which could also be described as looking very similar to a halo) were worn as a sign of sanctity or badge of royalty, by the gods and goddesses. Sometimes the stephane adorned the heads of a deity's priestesses and sacrificial animals to denote to whom they belonged or honoured.

The Latin for Goddess was *Dea*, such as Dea Roma, Goddess Rome, with the plural being *Deae*. *Deus* was the Latin for God, with the plural being di, dei or dii. Divus (male) or Diva (female) was a figure who has become divine, such as Romulus or a divinized king. Dea or Deus instead of Goddess or God, can be used as a title when working with, talking about, or invoking any deity from the Roman pantheon. The Romans also called the collective gods 'the blessed ones'. In the late Roman empire, it was known for the phrase *Nobiscum deus* meaning 'God with us' to be used as a battle cry but could also be used anytime one wished to invoke the divine to be present to act as a motivating or reassuring presence.

In the earlier period of Roman history, just as the gods were not personified, there was seen no need, and no attempt made, to relate the gods to one another in human-style relationships. The early Roman gods were mostly abstract. Therefore, there was no 'family of the gods' as such, nor genealogies. They were defined by the purpose or function they served for 'Rome' or their place or power in life and the cosmos, rather than being identified by their familial relations. They were sometimes depicted together when functioning within a certain theme or archetype; such as fertility and earthly abundance for Ceres, Venus and Fortune. In this case all three goddesses could be found depicted with the same symbols of the cornucopia, stalks of wheat or a globe, and given the title 'fruit bearer' in devotionals when they were embodying these aspects. However, it seems to be a later development to try to place the gods into family units and human relationships that reflected the ideals of domestic life that were so upheld in the Empire. Such a development is the marriage of Jupiter and Juno. Both of their earliest manifestations had associations with the sky and the heavens and so were joined together in a divine union. Jupiter and Juno came to be upheld as the ultimate example of martial felicity and faithfulness to emulate. There were many deities, however, that remained unconnected to or outside of the Jupiter family nucleus, such an example is Janus. All the gods were regarded by the ancient Romans to amplify, exemplify, and even favour many of the virtues of Roman life, such as duty, piestas (family devotion and loyalty), dignity and patriotism.

Sometimes it is argued by historians that this change to humanised or anthropomorphic Gods was perhaps also brought about by eastern or Greek influence. When a foreign deity (or its mythology) was affiliated or identified with a Roman one it was called *interpretation Romana* ('Roman translation'). Though it is very hard to sometimes decipher to what extent foreign deities were adopted by the Romans, often it seems that rather than the Romans adopting the deity, they merely equated them to their own to ease the amalgamation of the original culture or country into the Roman empire. Sometimes a foreign deity could be equated with several Roman deities, such as Athena, whom had similar aspects to Bellona, Minerva, Carmentis and Fortuna. The Roman Goddesses Salus, Albunea and Juturna were also all at some point associated with the British goddess Sulis and the Greek goddess Hygeia. They were connected through similar or shared themes, archetypes or attributes. It should be noted, however, that when a foreign god was equated with a Roman one, it did not indicate a belief that they were equal. The Roman deity remained the superior in status and it merely reflected the Roman practice of not challenging native beliefs and allowing foreign cultures to continue their worship and practices so long as their ultimate loyalty was the Roman state.

A deity could also be induced to change their loyalties or be transferred to 'Rome' via *evocatio*. Deities sometimes were promised better treatment in Rome and they could be induced to leave an area, such as happened with Goddess Cybele. When Rome conquered a country or people it was considered that their deities were also conquered or that a place could be conquered if its deities could be induced to leave via *evocatio*. Such an example if the *evocatio* of Juno Regina from the Etruscan city of Veii when it was conquered in 396 BCE.

In this chapter I keep to sharing the primary gods and goddesses of the city of Rome, those Italic gods that held principal place in the ancient religion of the city and whom the Romans would have deemed as part of the 'state religion'. To avoid confusion and excessive name-dropping I do not explore their affiliations, amalgamations or identifications with foreign gods.

Triads

Triad means a holy trinity and many times the ancient Romans and those before them grouped deities into triads, which were sometimes thematic and other times an indication of superiority or primary importance. Some historians have suggested that the association of certain triads with particular hills indicates the principal gods of the original villages or districts, and therefore cultures and heritage, that sat upon each of the seven hills of Rome.

The Archaic triad reflected the fact that the first Romans mostly lived by farming. Even when Rome became a vast city, rural life was still celebrated and Rome was very much dependant on the supplies of the country estates throughout the empire. The archaic triad was made up of Mars, an agricultural and fertility god and the more obscure Quirinus, connected to sacrifice and protection of the community, who later became associated with Romulus. In this triad, Mars and Quirinius were joined by either Jupiter, a weather god, who governed storms, lightning and rain or some argue it more likely that the third deity was originally Volcanus, also known as Vulcan, the God of Fire and metal-working. The triad had ancient links to the Palatine Hill.

There was also the Aventine Triad (also known as the Plebian triad) of the deities Ceres, Goddess of agriculture, harvest and crop growth, her son Liber, God of wine, freedom and fertility and Libera, daughter of Ceres and Goddess of vitality, springtime and grain. Their temple building was within a sacred district on Aventine Hill.

Later, historians speculate that it was in the early republic, influenced by the Etruscans, that the Capitoline triad, with their temple on Capitoline Hill became the principal gods of Rome and they were Jupiter, Juno and Minerva, in their aspects as Jupiter Optimus Maximus, Juno Regina and Minerva. Their Capitoline temple was said to have been built by King Tarquin following his war with the Sabines. There was also a shrine to the Capitoline Triad of Jupiter, Juno Moneta and Minerva on Quirinal Hill that is thought to pre-date the temple of Jupiter Optimus Maximus (6th century BCE).

Before the inclusion of Jupiter, however, the Etruscan Triad of Minerva and Juno previously included Juventas. Jupiter replaced Juventas upon his rise to supremacy (which in itself arguably reflected the rise of the patriarchy). Juventas was the maiden goddess of youth and rejuvenation and she was the maiden aspect of the divine feminine triad of Mother, Maiden, Crone. Minerva 'the wise or mindful one' represented the crone and Juno the mother – lover. In Etruscan culture women were considered equal status to men, with shared responsibilities and authority. Many Etruscan goddesses held supreme place in the Etruscan pantheon and were the patrons of the major cities and tribes. Tradition has it that the location of the Capitoline Temple was also home to other gods before it was built but these temples were moved to make room for Jupiter. However, Terminus, Mars and Juventas refused to move and so were incorporated into the new temple complex.

It is the principal Capitoline Triad of Jupiter, Juno and Minerva, whom I will share with you first and they reigned supreme during the majority of Roman history.

Chapter 8

The Capitoline Triad

The lofty pine is oftenest shaken by the winds; High towers fall with a heavier crash; And the lightning strikes the highest mountain.

Quintus Horatius Flaccus, also known as Horace (65 BCE – 8 BCE)

Jupiter

Jupiter came to be considered the highest of the Roman Gods and the ultimate example of kingship. He was originally a sky god associated with storms, rainfall, lightning and thunder and these associations did continue throughout Roman history. His primary place of importance can be contributed to his manifestation as rain; that essential element that enables to crops to grow, the rivers to flow and the earth to flourish. Jupiter was known for his benevolence, strength and wisdom and is frequently described as 'kindly disposed' towards humans. Clever and powerful he was respected as the mighty eagle, he who sees and knows all. He was closely connected to a God called Vediovis (or Vejovis), who was regarded as his opposite and personified all that was harmful, while Jupiter who was all that was good. His consort was considered to be Juno Regina and his son was Mercury, son of the sky.

In the earliest history of Rome, he was known as Jupiter Elicius *'he who brings forth'* and was associated with farming and the elements; the natural forces, like rain, that could destroy and create life. To the Latins and Etruscans, he was most well-known as the god who regulated rainfall and was evoked as such in many rites and rituals. According to Ovid, Jupiter was the god that created the seasons, splitting the year into four seasons, whereas before in the time of Saturn it has been a golden age of eternal spring. Jupiter's age was defined by silver, bronze and then iron. As the empire grew so did Jupiter's roles. He became the head of state as Jupiter Optimus Maximus (Best and greatest) and patron of the armies. War was declared under his aegis (breastplate or shield) and he was offered the spoils of war. Another popular epithet was Jupiter *Stator* 'Jupiter who holds men firm' (especially in the face of their enemy). The acronym IOM was used on almost all altars in dedication to the chief God of Rome, *Iuditer Optimo Maximo*. Many dedications were also made to him 'To Jupiter, Best and Greatest, who saves' in recognition of Jupiter as the supreme life sustaining power. Another popular name for Jupiter was Jove.

The temple of Jupiter stood on Capitoline Hill and was the largest and the most important in the city. It was recorded that in the regal era women of the aristocracy would climb the hill to his temple to pray for rain. Also, upon Capitoline Hill was the temple of Jupiter Feretrius the "maker of agreements" and it was Rome's oldest temple built in the eight century BCE. By tradition it was commissioned by Romulus to hold all his battle booty. On his feast day, the Ides of September (13th), every year, from the foundation of the republic onwards, a nail was hammered into the temple doorpost to mark the passage of time and remember the dedication of the temple. The Ludi Romani, the principal and grandest games of the year were celebrated in his honour annually mid-September, as were the Capitoline Games on 15th October and the Ludi Plebeii November 4th to 17th. These festivals coincided with the return of the rain after the drought of summer. Every year the consuls would also make a sacrifice to Jupiter to begin their term of office.

Bidentals were also sacred to Jupiter. A bidental is any place that has been struck by lightning. This was a practice inherited from the Etruscans, who walled in any area struck by lightning as it was deemed sacred space. To the Romans bidentals belonged to Jupiter alone (whereas the Etruscans believed many gods could communicate through various forms of lightning, such as Menvra the Goddess of lightning) and offerings were made to Jupiter in these locations. Two-year old animals were sacrificed to Jupiter at bidentals, two being symbolic of the two-pronged fork of lightning.

Juno

Juno was the supreme Goddess of the Roman pantheon and considered the Goddess of the People 'Juno *Populona'*. She was an Etruscan goddess of light, known to them as Goddess Uni and in ancient Lanuvium (Latium) as Juno *Sispes Mater Regina*; Juno, Saviour, Mother and Queen. There were many statues of her in the Etruscan capital of Veii which was considered her city as she was their patron. Livy tells us that when this city was sacked by the Romans many statues of her were taken to Rome and it was considered that she herself was also fully transferred at this time and officially became the patron of the Romans, as she had been previously for the Etruscans. However, she was present and worshipped from the earliest stages of Rome with her temple shrine built on the Esquiline Hill 735 BCE. For the Romans she was believed to be the majestic embodiment of the virtues of Roman matronhood. She was considered to be dignified, patient, modest, chaste and maternal, the virtues of all of which Roman women were encouraged to emulate. She was titled Juno Regina, Queen of Heaven and was the Goddess of marriage, motherhood and domestic harmony and the month of June was named in her honour.

She had ten different names that were associated with various themes, archetypes and festivals. As *Juno Lucetia/ Lucina* "the bringer of light" she was associated with moonlight and with childbirth. This was a very early aspect of Juno and it was believed she would safely bring children from the dark of the womb into the light just as the moon lights the way at night. Offerings to her were often made by women, in particular mothers and pregnant women as it was believed she would bestow nourishment and health. A grove to Juno Lucina was located on Esquiline Hill, where a temple was later built in 375 BCE. In the grove the vestal virgins would give offerings and locks of their hair that were hung upon a great and ancient tree. The consort of Juno Lucetia was Jupiter Lucetius, "Jupiter the bringer of light".

As goddess of light, heaven and the sky she was associated with several birds, including peacock and geese. Geese were guardians of household, farmland and the city of Rome, reflecting Juno's role of motherly protection. During the attack of the Gauls upon Rome in 390 BCE it was Juno's sacred geese that famously called the alarm and alerted the Romans to danger. As the guardian of the state and protective patron of the Eternal City, Juno was known as Juno *Moneto,* Juno, the 'One who Warns'. The temple of Juno Moneta crowned the Arx Capitolina and in the Area Capitolina was kept her sacred geese. She was also protectress of funds and Goddess of historical memory. In her temple buildings were kept the standards for weights and measures, as well as official lists of Magistrates and money was coined in her temple complex. Juno as Juno *Quritis* was of Sabine origin and had her own temple in the Campus Martius, where military functions, training and triumphs took place. Quritis (meaning spear, such as with the War God Quririnus) was the Sabine Goddess of protection, who guarded and watched over the people.

Juno, as great protectress and Goddess of light and motherhood has not only one source, but was worshipped by many early italic tribes including the Etruscans, Faliscans, Villanovans, Latins, Sabines and Umbrians. Some traditions in Latium, believed her to have originally been the consort of Vulcan, God of Fire, who was then later deposed by Jupiter. She was also mother and sole parent of the God Mars who was her son through union with a flower. As mother of Mars, she was also honoured as the grandmother of Romulus (Quirinus). She was also the mother of Iuventas 'youth'.

The kalends (the first) of every month were sacred to Juno. She also had several festivals, with the primary holy days considered to be on the 1st July and the 13th September.

Minerva

Minerva was the Etruscan goddess of wisdom, associated with weather phenomena. She was known to the Etruscans as Goddess Menvra and Menerva. In her Etruscan origins she was the child of both Goddess Uni and the God Tinia and known as "the lightning thrower" and was depicted by the Etruscans with lightning bolts as her primary symbol or personification. Menvra as the lightning bolt could illuminate the darkness of a storm and via light connected earth to heaven and it was this that led to her association with enlightenment and acquisition of wisdom and knowledge.

In ancient Rome she was the Goddess of health, art, learning, writing, crafts and trade guilds. It was believed that she would bless all those that sought to learn and create. She was associated with, and governed, writing, industry, craft, music and education and was known as *the goddess of a thousand crafts*. As Minerva was considered a Goddess of creation and construction, she was popular with, and patron of, craftsmen such as weavers, blacksmiths, metalworkers, bronzesmiths, artists, cloth and shoe makers, quarrymen and potters. She also presided over writers and was connected to clerks and libraries.

Minerva Medica was the patron of doctors and the cult of Minerva Medica was associated with healing and medical knowledge. As Minerva *Pallas* she was connected with weaving, spinning and domestic craft. Girls would make offering to her when they first began to learn spinning, winning and carding.

She was also considered a Goddess of song and music, in particular the flute.

On a coin created by Vespasian when he became Emperor of Rome, Minerva is shown over seeing a situation in which a female representing Rome is rising from the ground. The image is accompanied by the moot 'Roman Resurges' – 'Rome, thou shalt rise again'. It reminded all that saw it of Minerva's involvement in making Rome mighty through its craft and construction, and affirmed her as the Goddess who could bring things into being with the hands of men and inspire men to create and give life to thoughts and ideas.

The temple of Minerva in Rome on Aventine Hill, dedicated on the 19th March (pre-218 BCE), was the location of the headquarters for the guild of writers and actors and the guilds of craftsmen. Her statues were also frequently located in the libraries of the Roman Bathhouses and give tribute to the Roman interest in aligning physical culture and leisure with intellectual pursuits. Minerva was present wherever meetings, learning and the sharing and acquiring of knowledge could be conducted. As Minerva Capta ('captured'), she had a temple on the Caelian Hill in Rome which contained a statue of Minerva captured from Falerii. She also had a temple in the Forum of Nerva, built and dedicated by Domitian and a Temple of Minerva Medica on Esquiline Hill. She had her own temple as part of the Capitoline Triad complex on Capitoline Hill and was honoured there as part of the supreme triad of Rome.

Her main festival was the Quinquatrus on the 19th March, however, she also had festivals on the 19th June and the 13th September.

Minerva was the favourite Goddess of Emperor Domitian and he renamed the Chalcidicum of the senate house the Hall of Minerva in her honour. It was the courtyard from which one would enter all the rooms that housed records and important documents.

Chapter 9

Other Gods and Goddesses

In this chapter I will share with you the principal gods and goddesses of the Roman pantheon that together form the Di Consentes and the Di Selecti. It is believed that the selection of twelve deities for the Di Consentes was influenced by Etruscan religion. They themselves had twelve principal deities made up of six gods and six goddesses. The Romans reflect this with their twelve, though they chose some deities that were different to the Etruscan twelve.

Di Consentes

Di Consentes, meaning the consenting or harmonious Gods, comprised of twelve Roman deities, the Capitoline triad and an additional nine gods and goddesses. They were considered Jupiter's council.

In Rome could be found the Portico of the Di Consentes, that was next to the Clivus Capitolinus (one of the oldest and was significant streets in ancient Rome that led you from the Forum to Capitoline Hill) and near the temples of Saturn and Vespasian. This portico housed twelve gilt bronze statues of the twelve Di Consentes grouped in their traditional pairs (thought these were not marital pairs, except for Juno and Jupiter, but rather business or thematic collaborations); Jupiter and Juno, Apollo and Diana, Neptune and Minerva, Mars and Venus, Vesta and Vulcan and Mercury and Ceres. The earliest structure of this house for the gods was designed as if the deities were at a banquet in their honour, with a couch for each pair. When it was dedicated such a ceremonial meal was believed to have been conducted. Beneath the portico of the sacred twelve are unidentified rooms and behind it are seven small chapels.

Apollo

Apollo is believed to be an early Greek introduction to the Roman pantheon and this in a hope that he would ward of a devastating plague of the 5th century BCE. He was, however, already popular with certain Etruscan cities before the Romans officially recognised him. The Etruscans linked him with their Goddess Menvra and they were often linked in temple art and iconography. The Apollo of Veii (created 510-500 BCE) is arguably one of the most significant and spectacular Etruscans statues known to have existed and was created by the famous Etruscan sculptor Vulca. Given the high levels of Malaria in the city of Rome, that were greatly lamented by the physician Galen, combined with the high regard for prophecy in both Roman and Etruscan religion, it is not surprising Apollo was deemed an invaluable ally.

Apollo is a multifaceted god and to the Romans he was known as the god of harmony, plague and medicine, light and music, poetry and oracle. He was patron of the arts and the bridge between healing and prophecy. He was the personal patron of Emperor Augustus who built a temple to him on Palatine hill, near to the house of the emperor. This was a personal and political move that attempted to encourage the popularity of Apollo as a God of prophecy, especially when the prophecy favoured the expansion and might of Rome.

The first temple to Apollo, built in July 433 BCE, was built outside the sacred precincts of Rome, in the Campus Martius because he was a foreign god. Augustus's later temple, that of Apollo Palatinus housed the Palatine Library, the most significant of such in Rome and contained Greek and Latin collections of art as well as literature and the collection of Sibylline books; the books of prophecy compiled and channelled by his Sibylline priestesses. At another temple, the Temple of Apollo Medicus (Apollo the Healer), built in 431 BCE, games were held in his honour that always included music and theatricals. These games were repeated and became an occasion in his honour every 6th to 13th July. Later the theatre of Marcellus, built by Caeser and Augustus, was placed next to the temple and continued the celebration of written and spoken word and music. Augustus did much to revive the cut of Apollo. He was also the patron God of Emperor Nero and Nero dedicated to Apollo 1,808 crowns he had won for his performances in Greece.

His Laurel, that of the bards, poets and musicians, bound the hair of the Goddess Concord (of Harmony). It was likewise placed upon the heads of those that brought and maintained peace.

Ceres

Ceres was a Goddess of Agriculture, grain, fertility and the seasonal cycles, whose origins lie in early fertility cults. Mother to the god Liber and goddess Libe, her name derived from *creare*, meaning 'to create'. It is she that was believed to be the source of cultivated crops, as well as ensuring and supervising their growth and making the harvest bountiful. Cultivation is her speciality and Tellus Mater, Morth Earth receives the seeds that she sows. Ceres was also often a word or term given to grain or seeds themselves as a metonymy and spelt was the most common offering to her.

She was of primary importance in what was in origin an agricultural community, and she was also connected to the markets and cattle. She was a particularly favoured Goddess by the Roman plebians, the members of the lower social classes, such as the farm and land workers. She was also a Goddess of peace and the right of asylum was offered at her temple. Her temple, along with that of her two children, was on the Aventine Hill in Rome. At this temple grain was distributed to the poor.

Her priests were called Crearem, and she also had a flamen cerealis who was always a plebian. The same Flamen conducted rites for her two children and for Goddess Tellus. Her primary festival in April was the Cerialia which marked the beginning of the growing season. During this festival, white, her sacred colour, would be worn and all dark colours avoided in honour of the return of her daughter from the underworld. A pregnant *forda* cow (meaning fertile) was also sacrificed, symbolic of mother and daughter and it was a sacrifice in hope of a fertile agricultural year. The festivities concluded with the letting loose of a burning fox, to emulate an ancient story where a boy lit a vixen's tail and let it loose through the fields destroying the harvest.[14]

> *Let Earth and Ceres, mother of the crops, be propitiated with their own spelt, and with the entrails of a pregnant cow. Ceres and Earth maintain a joint duty: one gives the crops their origin, the other their place.*
> Ovid, *Fasti*, Book 1. 671

At harvest they would give the first fruits of spelt to Ceres in thanks. Ceres' cake was a very common offering at this time. An almost unique time of fasting[15] and silence was held in her honour on 4th October and she was sometimes associated with funeral rites and the underworld where her seed would enter to be given life.

Diana

Diana may have her origins as a nymph or spirit of the wild in Latin religious tradition. Diana was mostly a singular deity, though she was possibly once part of a Latin triad with Egeria (the woodland nymph associated with King Numa) and Virbius a Latin woodland deity that was worshipped alongside her at Nemi, their home. To the Romans she was the goddess of the wild, woodland and its beasts, as well as being associated with childbirth, fertility, maidens and the crescent moon. For the ancient Romans she came to be primarily associated with the protection of women, in particular young women and women experiencing or seeking pregnancy and childbirth. She may have had origins in the traditions of the italic tribes of the Latins, but eventually her cult spread very widely from her native Italy.

Within the city of Rome her primary temple was on the Aventine Hill, founded in the 6th century BCE and it was thought to have been built by, or for, the Latin league as a centre of worship. Here she was honoured as a goddess of fertility, childbirth and protector of the young. At this temple was displayed the skull of a sacred and beautiful cow that had been sacrificed to her soon after the temples construction.

She was also worshipped in several woodland groves and shrines. The most significant of these was the shrine, grove and spring just south of Rome, on the shore of Lake Nemi, with a temple that was founded later in the 8th – 7th century BCE. This woodland was sacred to her and none could hunt in it or cut down wood. The lake was known as the *speculum Dianae*, the mirror of Diana. Here she was known as Diana Nemorensis, 'Diana of the Woods'. The Appian way, that primary thoroughfare of out Rome led directly to this temple and lake and over time it grew into a large complex. It was protected by a single priest, who by tradition, was an escaped slave. There was an ancient contest at this shrine in which to become the priest one must kill the priest that came before. Her priest was named 'King of the Woods'. Diana had connections to the arts of healing and healing powers and this shrine became a centre of pilgrimage, especially in connection with fertility, conception, pregnancy and childbirth. Many votives have been found at the shrine in the shape of breasts, phalluses, and wombs. The Romans also believed and honoured this place as connected with the ancestors of Rome and the mythical stories and characters of the foundation of Rome and Alba Longa. It proved to be one of the most popular temples in central Italy.

Her crescent moon was believed to symbolise her presence and protection, and has been found depicted on the heads of many Roman children on their tomb reliefs and on other dedications associated with the young. Her feast day was the 13th August and was connected to harvest festivals at that time. Her festival was especially celebrated by slaves and her temple became a refuge for runaway slaves. Many of her processions, including that on her feast day that went from Rome to Nemi, involved a procession of flower garlands and torches; the torch, as shown in many of her statues, being her symbol of birth and renewed light.

Mars

Mars, was often known to the Romans as *Manius*. His cult and worship were considered second only to Jupiter's and his area of influence quite substantial. He was considered a dignified and noble Roman God, the divine example of the Paterfamilias. He most common epithet was Mars *Pater* meaning Mars the 'Father' and whereas Jupiter was considered the Divine King of Rome, Mars was considered the Father and Protector of the Roman people. He was known for his protection of land and farmers, though he also had connections to childbirth, children, parenthood, healing and fertility. When the farmers were called to defend their land as soldiers, he was believed to protect them then also. He would bring stabilisation where there was chaos and he represented actions and decisions to bring about peace.

His first noted beginnings are as an ancient Italian God of vegetation and land. He was considered the potent seed at the centre of all plants and flowers. He was a principal god of ancient Latium and also important to the Etruscans as a fertility god. For the Latins, Etruscans and Romans, Mars was connected primarily to fields and pastures, as well as the protection, fertility and vitality of the land and many aspects of farming. Throughout ancient Roman history he remained an agricultural deity with festivals linked to the agricultural year. He is most often mentioned or dedicated to in relation to the land, its creatures and the management of them, especially in Agricultural manuals, dedications and prayers, where he is called upon to make the plants grow, bring good health and protect livestock. He is also frequently linked with horses; horse breeding and horse races were held in his honour. His chief festival was the *Quinquatrus*, held around the spring equinox in March and marked the beginning of the agricultural year. At this time his priests, the *Salii*, would perform a leaping dance that was believed to help the corn grow. At the time of Cato the Elder (234 – 149 BCE) he was still considered the protector of the fields and Cato links him with an ancient ceremony of land purification.

He was the son of Juno and Juno alone. His conception came about when the Goddess Flora performed a ritual on Juno's behest and plucked a flower, before placing it upon Juno's belly. She was immediately pregnant and Mars was born from the great mother, by earthly conception and from thereon he remained connected to plant life and the feminine. He is born of the earth, and his birth was celebrated as the first of March, the month named in his honour and linked him with spring and the coming forth of nature[16]. He was also the father of Romulus and Remus, the founding fathers of the city of Rome, and so honoured as the father or paterfamilias of all Romans.

His most significant temple in Rome was the Temple of Mars *Ultor*, Mars the Avenger, which honoured his aspect as the protector of Rome. It was built by Emperor Augustus in celebration of his victory over Julius Caeser's assassins. It reflects that how by the time of the Roman empire Mars was evolving into a God of War and Battle, as Rome expanded so did the boundaries that Mars was requested to protect. His farmers staff became a spear, then a sword and shield, and sacrifices were made to him by the army before battle, and after victory.

He also had an altar in the Campus Martius (the field of Mars) and on the Appian Way. Just outside the city, there was temple dedicated to him on c.390 BCE as a God of fertility and farmers.

On the reliefs of the temple of Mars Ultor was Mars depicted with Goddess Venus and Eros on one side and Goddess Fortuna on the other, as well as Goddess Roma, the river Tiber and Romulus. Several artifacts with connections to war were held within the temple, such as Caesar's sword, and the forum of Augustus in front and surrounding the temple was full of statues of heroes such as Aeneas, Iulus and Romulus. Oxen was a frequent sacrifice to Mars, in recognition of him as the God of Agriculture and the plough.

Mercury

Known in ancient Rome as Mercurius, he was the god of profit, trade, travel, commerce and merchants. He was considered the son of the Goddess Maia and the God Jupiter and as Jupiter's son was considered God of the air and of abundance. He was often connected to luck and fertility charms and sometimes was even celebrated for military successes. As a God of prosperity, he was sometimes depicted with an oversized phallus, one of only a few gods to be so, with the phallus being regarded as a good luck and fertility symbol.

According to Ovid there was a spring of Mercury near the Porta Capena which was reputed to have divine power. In Rome his circular temple, with barrel vaulted roof, was on the Aventine Hill, and he shared the temple with his mother Goddess Maia. It was said to have been decorated with his sacred animals the cockerel and the ram and it was a centre for some guilds of merchants and traders. It is believed that it was dedicated in 495 BCE. However, this is the only known temple of Mercury in Rome and neither the temple, nor Mercury, were assigned a flamen, or priestly cast of his own. This may indicate that he is not one of the earliest or original gods of the city of

Rome. He seems to have been more popular in the empire than the city of Rome, perhaps reflecting his governance over travel and therefore those who travelled to and from the city and around the Empire.

The festival of Mercury was on the 15th May and guilds of merchants would feast on this day and visit his sacred spring to collect the waters. They might have made a prayer to Mercury such as the one shared by Ovid:

> *Just give me profits, give me joy when the profit's made, and*
> *make it a pleasure to have deceived the buyer!*
> Ovid, *Fasti*, V. 690 – 92

Neptune

Known to the Ancient Romans as Neptunus, he was an ancient God of Water, perhaps even the earth's water and reservoir itself. He was originally associated with rivers, fresh water and springs, as well as with moisture and soil. As such he would govern the fountains and the aqueducts and fresh sources of water to the city. He was particularly honoured at fresh water springs and it was common to make offerings to him there. Aqueducts were also considered sacred to Neptune. Varro considered Neptune's name to mean "the marriage of heaven and earth" referring to the waters that fell from the sky and became the rivers on the earth. The Etruscans named him Nethuns and it has been suggested that his name may stem mean 'damp' or wet'. In this form he is the morning dew and the moisture that is in the soil. During excavations of the Etruscan city of Vulci there was found the oldest depiction of Nethuns, dated to the fourth century BCE where Nethuns is kicking a rock and creating a spring from it.

He later also became the God of the sea, perhaps because all water eventually led to the sea. The cult of Neptune as God of the Sea was believed by some Romans to have been introduced to Italy by the hero Evander. He was also sometimes identified with the Roman God Consus and as a result became associated with horses, and was often depicted with his mythical sea creatures, such as tritons, hippocamps and nereids. As God of the Sea, he had associations with naval battle and even the colosseum which displayed its own naval battles! There was a particular style of Gladiator that used his Triton, a three-pronged spear of fishermen.

He had just one temple in Rome in the Campus Martius, built in 220 BCE. The temple was restored by the consul Gnaeus Domitius Ahenobarbus to commemorate his naval victory at Philippi over Gnaeus Domitius Calvinus.

Neptune had a festival on the 23rd July called the Neptunalia, which honoured him as a God of water sources in times of drought and heat. Offerings were made to him to ensure the return of fresh water supplies. At this time the constructs associated with water supplies such as drainage and basins were cleaned, conserved and maintained. He also had a festival on December 1st. Neptune was one of only three gods, Neptune, Mars and Apollo, to whom a bull was sacrificed.

Venus

Venus was a very early Italian vegetation spirit associated with spring, fertility, vegetation and plants. As a vegetation spirit or earth energy, it's original name and form was non-gendered and they encompassed both the male and female parts of plants. To the Etruscans they presided over the fertility of vegetable gardens, fruit and flowers. Their role involved into that of a fertility deity and is emphasised in the way that it was believed that it was Venus that taught the tree, plants, crops, birds and animals to come together and be joined in union. They gave the flowers and trees all of their reproductive parts. Later, they came to be regarded as a Goddess and was believed to govern a broader understanding of fertility, vitality and fecundity, which incorporated the sensuality, pleasure and beauty of nature and reproductive potentiality and creativity. Many Roman poets evoked her in their works, including Lucretius and Catullus.

In the *Aeneid* Virgil had Venus as the mother of Aeneas, the trojan prince, who descendants founded Rome. During the tale she sends her pair of doves to guide him to the golden branch that he seeks. Julius Caeser, and after him Augustus, also claimed Venus Genetrix, through Aeneas, as his divine ancestor to validate his right to rulership. His building of a temple to her in 46BCE greatly increased her popularity. In 135 CE the emperor Hadrian also build a significant temple in her and Goddess Roma's honour. In the temple the statue of Venus faced east and Roma faced west. This temple celebrated Venus as the divine ancestress of both Rome and specifically the Julian family. In the Aeneid Venus is described as the daughter of Jupiter, while other sources have her as a child of Tellus Mater, Mother Earth. On the 1st of April the Romans celebrated the Veneralia in honour of Venus and some associated this month with her.

As Venus Cloacina "Venus the Purifier" she was also a goddess of cleanliness, self-care and hygiene, bathing and domestic living was connected to her. In this way she was connected to the creation and maintenance of beauty and purification, and could be found depicted from mosaics in the home to statues in the bathhouses. She was also the patron goddess of Pompeii.

Vesta

Vesta was the Goddess of the Household Hearth, as well as the eternal flame and hearth of Rome and its empire. Her warm and fiery self also governed sown fields and she was considered a Goddess of vitality that sparked and sustained life. Unlike other Roman deities, there was no statue of her within her temple. She was perhaps considered the most omnipotent of the gods as she was the literal hearth place and fire, with no human form until much later in Roman history. She is considered to be a Goddess from ancient Latium, who was the centre of the domestic fire cult. Her name means: 'to stand by force', meaning 'that is exists and is standing due to its own force' i.e. it is no dependant on another or anything, self-sourced.

The house of Vesta was located in the Forum Romanum and her shrine was attended by six vestal virgins, who remained in her service for thirty years. They were expected to remain virgins in this time in order to fulfil their role of continuously tending and maintaining the eternal flame. The shrine of Vesta was a circular shape and Plutarch gives its shape a symbolic and poetic significance and says that the circle represented the eternal fire at the centre (Vesta) with the universe surrounding it. The eternal, or living flame within her temple was considered literally to be Vesta manifest, not just symbolic of. The priestesses would keep this flame alight and in doing so kept the Goddess present in Rome, protecting the city. The extinguishing of this fire would mean the destruction of the nation.

Vesta was also connected to many households' religious observances and rites of passage and in the home, she was worshipped alongside the Lares and the Penates. She was also the hearth fire of the home, where food was cooked and warmth given. Like the eternal flame the household hearth was always kept alight. The Romans believed that a cold hearth meant an uninhabited house, a very unlucky omen. Libations of wine were poured on the hearth fire every day and a portion of the food from the evening meal was offered. For rites of passage, the veil and dress of a bride was red, orange or yellow in her honour and offerings were made to her on the wedding day, for peace and happiness in the home. Such was her importance that sacrifices and prayers were often concluded with her name.

Vulcan

Vulcan is an ancient Latin deity, with one of his earliest names being Volcanus. He is often considered one of the oldest gods known to have been worshipped in Italy, and like Vesta, connected to the Cult of the Fire. As Volcanus, he was a principal God in Latium, possibly with his consort being Juno, before Jupiter displaced him. He later continued in his role of a protector of Rome and by tradition he was a favoured God of Romulus, whom dedicated a temple to him, the *Vulcanul*, one of the first in the new city. In was in this temple that Romulus chose to place a statue of himself being crowned by victory. After the battle with the Camerians Romulus also dedicated a bronze four horse chariot to the temple and he chose to end his Triumph's here in honour of the god.

He was God of the volcanoes, earthquakes, of fire, fertile land and possibly also patron of those that used fire for craft, such as blacksmithing and metalwork. It was his essence and lava that made the soil rich and fertile. He had his own flamen, the flamen Volcanalis and an additional temple in the Campus Martius. The sacred black stone of the Forum was also connected to Vulcan and his worship. His festival of Vulcanalia was celebrated on the 23rd August, when the heat of the summer was at its greatest peak. Offerings were made to request the prevention of fire and drought. He was also venerated as the chief or patron deity of Ostia, the port town of Rome.

In Rome's mythology Vulcan was the father of Cacus, a monster who lived in a cave in a mountain that spewed fire and smoke. Cacus terrorized the people of Rome. During the time of Evander, Hercules was as said to have visited the area and defeated Cacus, making Rome liveable from thereon. In other earlier Etruscan stories Cacus, son of Vulcan, was a renown Seer, blessed with the sight. Sight and oracle were also frequently connected to fire and Vulcan and there are votive offerings that have been found dedicated to Vulcan in the shape of eyes.

His consort was considered to be the Goddess Maia, who gave her name to May growth of living things and fertile land.

Di Selecti

The Di Selecti are the twenty principal gods of the Roman religion. They are all the deities included so far and these additional eight.

Genius

Genius literally translates as 'begetter'. He is a God very much personifying an archetype or divine aspect. He was considered to be both a singular divine form or entity himself and could also manifest as an aspect that could reside within physical beings and forms.

The God Genius who was a singular divine entity was personified as Genius Publicus Populi Romani, which means 'the spirit of the community of the Roman people'. His shrine was located in the Forum Romanum where an annual sacrifice was made to him at his festival on the 9th October. He was depicted as a bearded male figure draped in a cloak who was holding a cornucopia or a *patera* (libation bowl). In the imperial age he came to be depicted with a crown, globe and spectre as well as cornucopia, perhaps reflecting Rome as the centre of an Empire. He held the power of generation, vitality and virality and held the potency that enabled a man to have children.

Throughout the Empire there was also the Genius *Cucullatus* who were 'the hooded spirits', often depicted as a giant or a dwarf carrying a bag of money, eggs or a scroll. *Cucullatus* referred to the type of cloak they were depicted wearing. They were also depicted with or as phallic symbols and were associated with fertility, prosperity, rebirth and renewal.

Additional to this was the Genius that was a man's guardian spirit and, or, the divine aspect or essence of the masculinity that connected it to the divine itself. Genius was an immortal part of any male individual and you could call it 'The Divine Masculine' aspect of all men. Some have equated it to the concept of a soul, although the Romans deemed the soul to be a separate aspect of self, called the Manes. The Genius of a man was considered by the Romans to be his vital, generative force, while the manes was the part of Self that embodied their essential character and personality. In this form Genius was often depicted as a snake (his female equivalent was called the Iuno/Juno). The Roman writer, Horace, said that only the genius knows what makes one person different from another and it is a god who is born and dies with each one of us.

The idea of genius also extended to refer to a guardian of groups, places and areas. These were called the genii or genius loci. Just as the genius presided over an individual man, so that genii would preside say over a particular grove of trees or a river. There could also be a genius *Patriae*, which was the spirit of the country. All genii were divine and needed to be properly worshipped and respected.

It was made compulsory by the senate that at every formal private and public dinner a libation was given in offering to the genius Augusti, the spirit or genius of The Emperor (not a specific emperor but the genius that resided in all Emperor's while they served as such).

Janus

Janus was an ancient Italic God who was popular with not just the Romans but throughout Italy, long before the beginning of the republic. In Rome his cult was believed to have been established in Rome by Romulus, the founder of Rome and so he is traditionally one of the oldest known Roman deities to have been worshipped there. His name regularly appears first in lists of deities in prayers, even in some cases taking precedence over Jupiter or Mars. He would also always receive the first portion of a sacrifice. It was traditionally believed that he was the first born from, or made from, the original Chaos and was the doorway for creation itself. Under the name Janus *Pater*, Janus the Father, he was known as the god of creation. It was also believed by some ancient Romans that Janus had ruled an age that pre-dated or followed the rule of Jupiter. His kingship was considered *the* catalyst for the turning of the ages.

He was honoured as a great guardian of not just Rome, but of the whole universe and was celebrated as the God of new and good beginnings. He was most well known as *Janus Bifrons*, 'two faced' and his two faces looked forwards and backwards, or east and west. As God of doorways, gates, entrances and exits and the public gates of roadways, he saw in and out, forward and back and presided over thresholds of all kinds. He carried a great key, as well as a virga or stick that was for protecting and defending those that meant to intrude or cross boundaries unwanted. He was associated with safety, order and peace.

As well as protecting and being present at the gates to the city of Rome, he also had his own temple, that of Janus *Geminus*. This shrine was originally located in the Forum Romanum. The gate to this temple was called 'The Gate of War' and was opened in times of war, so that there was a way to return and closed in times of peace, so that peace could not escape. The gates were said to have remained closed for forty-three years during the reign of King Numa, the longest length of time in Roman history. He was also the god of transitions, and he inspired the month of January, named for him and the first day of each month was sacred to him. On the 1st of January he was particularly venerated and this day was marked by the exchanging of oil lamps that would light and mark the passage forward of the year to come. Also, on this sacred day of Janus the army would reaffirm vows to the gods, who in exchange would continue their protection of Rome, and the consul also entered office on this day. Ovid writes of saffron being burnt for Janus on New Year's Day.

His consort was said to be Goddess Carna, the Goddess of hinges, who had the power to open what was closed and close that which was open. One of his children became the deity Tiber, of the River Tiber, who guarded that threshold.

Liber

Libations were said to have been introduced by Liber and he was the first to offer libations to Jupiter. Ovid believed this to be the origin of Liber's name. He was also known to the Romans as Liber Pater, referring to him as 'Liber the Free Father' and was the God of viticulture, freedom and male fertility. As Liber Pater he has associations with free speech and the rights of free men. As such he became connected to the coming of age of boys, when as a man they would gain their legal rights and be able to marry and father children. Liber was also a god connected to agriculture and corn, and it was believed that he protected corn. He also discovered honey and thereafter cultivated it and shared the knowledge of this cultivation, as he had also done with the vine.

Liber's temple on Aventine Hill, was that which was built for the Aventine Triad; Liber, Ceres and Libera. It was built in 496 BCE and dedicated in 493 BCE. Liber was considered to be the son of Ceres, the grain mother. They were known as the triad of the Plebs and Liber became a God associated with plebeian commoners who were the working classes of ancient Rome.

Liber is often thought to have been equated with the god Dionysus. The Romans called Dionysus, God of wine and revelry, Bacchus. However, during the late republic, the introduction of the cult and worship of Dionysus-Baccus shocked the city and many times, such as in the 1st century BCE the cult, worship and rites of Dionysus-Bacchus were banned due to its 'wild rites'. Liber had a more dignified and restrained character than Baccus and the cult of Dionysus was looked upon with the same suspicion as many eastern gods and condemned as encouraging social unrest and degraded behaviour.

Liber and Libera shared a festival, Liberalia, on March 17th where there were songs, sacrifices and a custom of hanging masks upon trees. This festival was connected to his discovery of honey and his introduction of libations. The festival was presided over by an elderly female priestess and on this day throughout Rome elderly women would be dressed with ivy crowns, to indicate that they were priestesses of Liber known as the Sacerdos Liberi. These priestesses would make his honey cakes and makes sacrifices to him. At this festival many boys would also celebrate their coming of age. Liber itself in Latin can also mean 'free' and during the Liberalia the toga was presented to boys that came of age. The toga symbolised that the boy now had the status of a free citizen and they would symbolically remove their bulla.

Luna

Luna was literally the personification of the moon. The moon Goddess was considered to actually be the fire or the light of the moon. Varro considered her one of the 'visible gods' along with Sol, Vesta and others that could be physically seen by humans. The Roman writer, Horace. titles her "two-horned queen of the stars" and Luna was often represented driving a two-yoke chariot (biga) which was drawn by horses or oxen. Her sacred animal was these oxen that pulled her chariot and sometimes she was referenced just by the symbol of horns as an upward facing crescent. She was frequently paired with Sol, who drove a four-horse chariot (quadriga) and she had a sibling Aurora, who was the Goddess of the Dawn. She was connected to agriculture and honoured in her connection to the marking the passage of time and the seasons. For the ancient Romans it was a sacred practice to sow, plant and harvest under certain and appropriate phases of Luna's cycle. She was considered to be one of the most ancient goddesses whose worship was important in the early days of Rome and into the time of the kings, though veneration of her seemed to decrease during the middle of the imperial age, as it did for Sol. The name Luna seems to be of Sabine origin.

There were other goddesses in the Roman pantheon that were connected to stages or aspects of the moon, such as Juno and Diana, and they were given her name as an epithet. However, Luna encompassed all phases and all aspects of the moon and she was believed to be the very essence of both the planet and the idea of moonlight. Sometimes she was depicted as part of an aspect of a moon goddess triad which included Diana and Proserpina.

Tacitus shares in book 15 of his *Annals* that in myth and legend a great altar and shrine was raised to her by the hero Evander. There were at least two temples in her in Rome. One was located on Aventine Hill and was built by King Servius Tullius, and dedicated on 31st March (pre 2nd century BCE). This hill seems to have been particular connected to agricultural cults and worship. There was another a temple to Luna Noctiluca, 'Luna that shines by night' on Palatine Hill. Luna also shared a temple with Sol (The Sun) which was located in the Circus Maximus. She has festivals on the 31st March and 24th and 28th August. On the 28th August Luna was worshipped alongside Sol in the Ludi Circenses. Monday was also considered a holy day to Luna and was named in her honour.

Orcus

All three titles and names Dis, Orcus and Plouton were commonly used to refer to the Lord of the Underworld. Orcus, was an Etruscan name in origin and he was the god of the underworld though the term Orcus was also used as a name for the underworld itself. He was often identified with the Sabine God Soranus. Orcus was commonly depicted in Etruscan funerary art as a bearded giant. As Orcus he was punisher of broken oaths and governed the purification of deceased souls. Orcus had no official cult in the city but his presence continued in rural areas after the Etruscan period.

Pluto, our modern abbreviation, was known to the ancient Romans as Plouton, meaning 'mineral wealth'. Plouton was one of the titles or epithets given to the Lord of the Underworld and refers to his aspect as the God of wealth and riches; all of the minerals, riches, crystals, gems that lay beneath the earth. He was also known to the Romans as the God Dis (also Dives), meaning "rich", or Dis Pater "father of riches" referring to the god of the underworld and the dead, also as the father of the richness of minerals and underground fertility that resulted in the richness of agricultural land.

Again, as with many deities he had many links with the seasons and agriculture. Whether named or honoured as Orcus, Plouton, or Dis he was considered a god of the fields, though primarily the ground itself; the ground into which we all ultimately go and from which all life ultimately comes from. It was believed that oaths, prayers and devotions could reach him by the hitting the ground with your hands and this was the way in which he was generally invoked.

There may have been a temple of Orcus on Palatine Hill but no physical evidence remains. There was once a vaulted underground pit, the Mundus, that connected the city of Rome with the gods of the underworld in which rituals were conducted. However, no archaeological evidence has ever been found, therefore its location is unknown. There has, however, been found an altar to Dis discovered on the edge of the Campus Martius near the River Tiber. It was believed that this marshy location was a point of communication with the underworld and offerings were made here where possibly vapour was once emitted from a small volcanic fissure. Caves may also have been a ceremonial space for connection to Orcus.

A common sacrifice to him was a black sheep and the colour black in general was associated with the rich fertile earth.

Saturn

Saturn was said to have been the original God (or Divine King) of Latium and ruled Italy during a golden age of peace, prosperity and abundance[17]. It was an age when the land was always in the season of spring, an age before Jupiter. In Saturn's time Goddess Justice, the maiden (who became the constellation of Virgo) was present among the people. At this time, it was said that the land of Latium had the name Saturnia. He was an ancient nature deity, who introduced agriculture to the ancient people and then went onto govern agricultural in all its aspects. His name may mean 'stuffed' or 'sowing', and may come from the term *satur/ satus,* which reminded Romans of his links to abundance, fertility, crops and land. It has also been suggested that his Etruscan name *satre* or *satria,* means 'the god whom the Satre clan worship'. As the god of seeds, sowing and agricultural seasons he was associated with Ops, the Goddess of grain and grain storage. He was said to be the father of Picus, the Roman God of Farming. He was often depicted with the symbol of a ship as in his mythology he was said to have travelled the great oceans of the world before finally arriving in Latium[18] where his golden reign commenced.

Saturn's temple was one of the earliest founded in Rome, being built in the late 6th century BCE, on the site of an earlier 7th century open shrine and altar. Both were located in the Forum Romanum, at the base of Capitoline Hill. The sanctuary and then late temple were home to a wooden statue of Saturn, an appropriately organic material and it was said to have had its feet wrapped in wool. The temple also held a state treasury of law and financial documents in its basement and the standards of the Roman legions. In true Saturn style, as the lord of time and matter, who controls its limits and structures, the Emperor

Augusts, in 20 BCE set up a column at the foot of the staircase leading to the temple and the column was considered the centre or *umbilicus* of Rome. Upon the column was inscribed in bronze, the distant from Rome to all the principal cities of the Empire. Tiber Island is also by tradition deemed to have been formed by the dumping of corn into the river; that is, the corn that because it had been grown on sacred land and was therefore unconsumable, had been offered up to Saturn and Ceres.

Saturn was known as Father time and this aspect of him was celebrated with the festival of Saturnalia, centred around the 17th December. This festival marked the end of the autumn seed sewing and was originally a festival of the farmers. He was a God of responsibility, systems and structure; the seasons only passed because of his turning wheel. However, during this festival freedom was celebrated, restrictions relaxed and ordinary rules were turned on their head; masters could serve their slaves and food was eaten out in the open at large banquets.

Sol

Sol was the Roman Sun God. For the early Romans he was literally the personification of the sun and worshipped as a solar deity. He was also known as Sol Indiges (the "native son") perhaps to define him from the later Sol Invictus. The crown of solar rays, or halo, became his symbol. The worship of Sol in Rome was said to have been introduced not long after the foundation, by the Sabine King Titus Tatius. There was a temple of Luna and Sol on the Circus Maximus in Rome built in the 1st century BCE. It was believed that this temple was built on the site of an earlier shrine to Sol, created by King Titus himself. Both Sol and Lunar's festival was held on 28th August. It is known that a ceremonial dance of the sun was performed at his temple in which men and women wore golden headdresses decorated with precious jewels and gold filigree. On August 9th an annual sacrifice was offered to Sol Indiges at his shrine on Quirinal Hill.

The time of the Empire saw the introduction of the undefeated or unconquered son or Sol Invictus and was the focus and deity of a Syrian solar cult that had connections to Mithraism. He rise in the 2nd century CE led to the gradual decline of the worship of Sol. Sol Invictus was considered the bringer of light to all men and the temples were noted as being circular. In the reign of the emperor Aurelian (270-5 CE) Sol Invictus became the centre of imperial worship and a new temple, with a new collage of priests, was built on December 25th, which then became Sol Invictus's official festival day and a national holiday for all citizens of the empire. December 25th was from then on considered by the ancient Romans the birth day of Sol, the holy sun. Sunday was originally named in honour of Sol and then later also associated with Sol Invictus.

In the time of the Empire Sol became linked to the emperors. Constantine and Nero were just two of the emperors that were depicted as the sun God in statue or reliefs. In one of these depictions Constantine as the Sun God rises from the sea in his chariot drawn by four horses. Sol was made the chief deity of Rome by the Emperor Elagabalus (Reign 218 -222 CE). He was a priest of Sol Invictus El Gabal and named himself in honour of the deity.

Tellus

Tellus literally means earth. The Romans worshipped two Goddesses of the earth; Tellus and Terra, though often the names were used interchangeably. Tellus Mater was Mother Earth and she was the personification of the receptive and productive power of the earth. She was also a goddess of fertility, marriage, agriculture and earthquakes. She is often shown depicted with animals and children. In the land and fields, Tellus was considered to work in union with Goddess Ceres. The Goddess Ceres would specifically govern the grain, watching over the seed through all stages, from planting to picking. She worked alongside Tellus Mater (Mother Earth) who brought blessing to the soil and would give life to the seed when it was planted in her body.

Many depictions and representation of Tellus Mater are found in funerary art and burials as it was believed that life after death was a descent of the physical body into her maternal arms and a re-union with the great mother. The depictions often include images such as bones or ashes transmuting or giving birth to flowers.

Her temple in Rome was dedicated in 268 BCE on Esquiline Hill and saw the meeting of the Senate the day following the assassination of Julius Ceaser.

In Rome there was an agricultural festival of Tellus held on 15th April called the Fordicidia. During the festival of Sementivae (January 24th – 26th when seed sowing began) in order to promote the fertility of the fields and cattle, in each of the thirty wards (areas) of Rome a pregnant cow was sacrificed to her. The ashes of the cow's unborn calf were used by the vestal virgins for a purification rite in another festival. She also had another festival on the 13th December, the date on which her temple was dedicated.

Part III

Chapter 10

Your Practice

If you have a garden and a library, you have everything you need.
Marcus Tullius Cicero. Roman Orator, Politician
and Historian (106 – 43 BCE)

There is a saying *'All that stands is Roman, all that moves is Greek'*. This hints at the gifts and lessons that can be received through connection and communion with ancient Rome, its deities and ideas.

Rome was all about solid structures, having and building firm foundations so that from that place one can rise with the most powerful growth. Potential and legacy are the vibrational words and essence that the Roman pantheon offer us to work with. Therefore, the Roman pantheon are here for you when you need support, guidance and wisdom in establishing foundations of any kind and when you wish to create or build something that is strong and sustainable, whether it be a relationship, a business, a home or a movement. They will support you in remembering who you are and why, and where and what you have come from. From this solid, centred and grounded knowing, the energy and spirit of Rome will support you in discernment about your choices, helping you to align with your truth and what helps you to best serve humanity, the divine and the cosmos. The expansive energy of the Roman pantheon will inspire you to expand into your greatest potential and open to considering and exploring all the possibilities of you.

In this chapter I share with you some practices, tools and ideas that you can use to integrate the Roman pantheon into your life and how they can inspire you in embodied living.

We begin at the nucleus, just as Rome grew up and out from seven hills. At the core of Rome are the mighty and the powerful principal deities of Rome, the Capitoline Triad.

Connecting to the Capitoline

The Capitoline Triad of Rome are Jupiter, Juno and Minerva, and they represent or embody the qualities of Benevolence, Devotion and Wisdom and Father, Mother and Wise Woman.

These are the three pillars that will both hold up your connection to the Roman pantheon and will facilitate the greatest gifts you will receive and lessons you will learn. Think of these three deities as a temple building itself:

Minerva as the platform, that solid grounding in wisdom and embodiment of Self and the foundational principles of alignment and knowing. With her learn, practice and seek to understand fully and discern your why and how so that you can create from firm roots. *'Know thyself'*

Juno as the columns, that represent the containing, compassionate and protective arms of the divine. She teaches devotion to unification and integration. With her learn to devote yourself to your sacred marriage and union within, so that you can then bring the healing of that same, outside of ourselves. *'Love Thyself'*

Jupiter as the ceiling, reminding us that with our feet firmly planted in truth and embodied wisdom, and loving held by compassion and respect, we can and must, then reach and aspire to our fullest potential. He will teach you that like the sky, you are limitless and anything is truly possible. *'Trust Thyself'*

They can also be represented by the three symbolic colours of ancient Rome.

Gold – Juno (Devotion, Union, Sovereignty)
Purple – Jupiter (Responsibility, Self-authority, Aspiration)
White – Minerva (Learning, Discernment, Discipline)

These three deities were invoked even when other deities were being addressed, in respect to their supremacy. You may want to include them in any Roman altar, ritual, prayer you create. Invoke them by name, or you can represent them with the colours suggested or reflect on their themes and wisdom and discern something that to you symbolises their aspects. You could also use the invocation I created for them in the next section.

Music and Dance

Musical instruments were played to accompany religious rituals, as well as public games, banquets, funerals and as signals in the army. Music was thought to drown out the sounds of ill-omen. Girls from wealthy families also had music lessons at home, in instruments such as the cithara. On the Ideas of June (13th) pipe players would play parading through the city before assembling at the temple of Minerva, as Minerva was credited with creation of the long pipe. She was also the first to play it, but seeing how it buffed out her cheeks, she threw it into the river and it was found by a faun. The trumpet was connected to Vulcan and it was believed that he was the god that first created it. This connection was celebrated at the Tubilustrium, the ceremony of the purification of the trumpets used in sacred rituals.

We also know that there was dancing involved in some religious observances and priests such as the *Corybantes* (in service of Magna Mater) and the *Salli* of Mars both used dance in their rituals. The Arval priests of Dea Dia also used dance in her festival of grain and cereal crops in May. Livy also records that there was a rope dance offered in worship of Juno that was performed by maidens. Many dances seem to have been influenced by, or inherited from the Etruscans, who used and enjoyed dance in their social and religious activities. There was even a dance that was specifically attributed to Romulus. It was believed that he created the Bellicrepa, a dance that was taught to Roman soldiers. Professional dancers could also be hired by wealthy Romans and Domitian and Nero were both well known for including them in their entertainments. Many of the dances seemed to have utilised the universal moves of circles, spirals, jump steps, swaying, figure of eights and weaving, with a lifting and undulating of arms.

You may want to listen to the instruments and music of ancient Rome as a way to connect to the Roman gods. Use music also for meditation, ritual, dance or reflection. The double flute, cymbals, pipes, rattles, tambourines, horns, trumpets and lyre were used by the ancient Romans for celebration and religious occasion. The *cornu*, a large curved horn was most commonly played on these occasions.

Carmen (from which the modern word charm derives) was the Latin word for 'song, chant, or prophecy' and when you use music, song, dance or poetry in your ritual, ceremony, worship or invocation you may want to invoke, give particular thanks or make an offering to Carmentis, the Goddess of Prophecy and sacred word, or The God Apollo, the inventor of music and poetry.

Talismans

Here are some ideas for symbols or shapes that you may want to wear as a follower of the Roman pantheon, or to connect to energy or essence of ancient Rome and, or its deities. Use these as a Talisman, necklace, body or dress adornment, to wear daily or in ritual or ceremony. You can also add them to an altar as a sacred object.

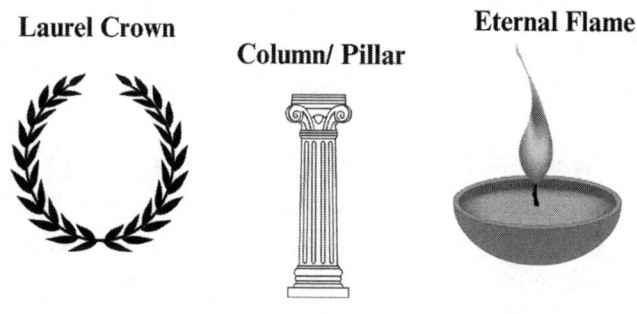

Laurel Crown

Column/ Pillar

Eternal Flame

Roman Pantheon Symbols

She- Wolf

Stork

Cornucopia

Roman Pantheon Symbols

Laurel – Symbolic of embodying your inner emperor/empress, sovereignty, leadership, rhetoric, wise thinking and wise speaking, discernment, self-responsibility. In particular use this symbol for connection to, or in honour of, the Capitoline Tria; Jupiter, Juno and Minerva, or Apollo, The Muses and Victory.

She-Wolf of Rome – Symbolic of ferocity, loyalty, determination, motherhood, loving devotion. Lupa also represents legacy and destiny and invites you to seek, understand and actualise your truth, your essence, your divine purpose and destiny.

Pillar – Symbolic of strength, stability, solidity, continuity, legacy, structure, building/growth, divine communion, embodiment, or, your body, home or sacred space as a temple.

Cornucopia – Symbolic of abundance, fertility, prosperity, life, growth, nature. Also, one of the symbols of Roman Goddesses Fortuna, Abundantia, Ceres, Pomona, Tellus Mater and Ops.

Flame – Symbolic of the Eternal Flame of Vesta. Use the symbol to remind yourself of the eternal flame that is within; that your hearth may burn warm and welcome all with respect and compassion and that you may live with devotion and passion to your dreams, to your heart and in service to the all.

Stork – To represent Pietas; duty to the divine all in all things, through respectful and dutiful action. The stork returns to the same nest each year and takes care of its parents in old age. Therefore, it was deemed a prime example of filial piety.

Affirmation and Invocation.

In this section I have included both ancient invocations or speeches to some deities of the Roman pantheon written by Roman writers and a modern invocation to the Capitoline Triad created by myself with the support of the deities themselves.

You are invited to use either or choose which resonates most! Or even mix them up and add your own words or use these as starting points for your own art, poetry, affirmations or for deepening connection as a repeated mantra.

Invocations and affirmations can also be used as prayers, to open space in ritual or ceremony or as part of an activity, meditation or journalling time. They can be read aloud, in your head or written as a sacred act. Remember that your voice is an offering to the gods! Words are just as valuable, perhaps more so than grains or incense, because they come from within you, are sourced in your body, heart and soul. So, speak with intention and awareness of the power of your words to destroy and to create, and speak with devotion, reverence and honesty.

You do not need to use the Latin anytime it is given but you may wish to if you feel comfortable with that.

Shorter Phrases

Roman words or phrases you could use as affirmation, in ceremony or ritual:

> *Bona fide* – In good faith, genuine. Use as a declaration of your honest intent.
> *Carpe Diem* – Enjoy the present or seize the day, first used by Horace to encourage you to life your life to the fullest.
> *Semper Fideli* – Always faithful.
> *Aere perennius* – More lasting than bronze, as in 'my love/ devotion is…'
> *Amor Vincit Omnia* – Love conquers all things, a phrase credited to Virgil.
> *Id est* – 'It is' Which could be used at the end of an invocation instead of 'and so it is'
> *Ad astra per aspera* – Through adversity to the stars. Use to remind yourself that you are capable and to trust in the support and guidance of divine.
> *Ad Meliora* – Toward better things.
> *Lupus non timet canem latrantem* – A wolf is not afraid of a barking dog. Use with Lupa, Bellona and Mars when you need a boost of courage, confidence or tenacity!
> *Dii Propitii* – May the gods be favourable.

Ancient Roman

These invocations, prayers and poems are from ancient Roman sources and were used by the Romans themselves. Some are from texts; some are well-known sayings and others are from devotionals or dedications of various sources. You can use them as they are or add to them as part of a ritual, ceremony or meditation. When you speak these words, you are speaking the words of the past and bringing them forth for modern embodiment and worship.

Tellus Mater

Holy Goddess Earth, Nature's mother, who bringeth all to life, and revives all from day to day. The food of life Thou grantest in eternal fidelity. And when the soul hath retired we take refuge in Thee. All that Thou grantest falls back somewhere into Thy womb.

Roman prayer to Mother Earth, second or third century BCE

The Divine

Changes of shape, new forms, are the theme which my spirit impels me now to recite. Inspire me, O gods, it is you who have transformed my art, and spin me a thread from the world's beginning down to my own lifetime, in one continuous poem.

The prologue of Ovid's *Metamorphosis*

Diana

Dianae sumus in fide,
Puellae et pueri integri:
Dianam pueri integri,
Puellaeque canamus.

O Latonia maximi,
Magna progenies Ioius,
Quam mater prope deliam,
Deposiuit oliuam,
Montium domina ut fores
Siluarumque uirentium,
Saltuumque sonantum:
Tu Lucina dolentibus
Iuno dicta pueperis,
Tu potens Triuia et notho es

Dicta lumine Luna.
Tu cursu, dea, menstruo
Metiens iter annuum,
Rustica agricolaw bonis
Tecta frugibus expels.
Is quocumque,
Tibi placet:
Sancta nominee,
Romulique,
Antique ut solita es, bona
Sospites ope gentem.

We faithful children,
Are loyal to you Diana.
Diana let us sing,
We your loyal children.
O child of Latona,
Great daughter of the greatest Father,
Whom your mother birthed
By the Delian olive tree,
Mighty lady of the mountains and green woods,
And hidden glens
And roaring rivers;
You who are called Mother of the Grove of light
May you bring ease to Mothers in childbirth,
You who are called mighty Trivia (lady of the crossroads),
Reflect your moon light upon us as we meet.
You, Goddess, who measure out the monthly cycle,
The circuit of the year,
So that it is full of good fruits
And fills the homes of farmers and growers.
By all of your holy names,
Bless us with goodness and keep us safe
as you have always done,

For the race of Romulus.

Catullus, Carmen, 34 (1st century BCE) ~ *Hymn to Diana,*
Roman Goddess of Maidens, the crescent moon and the Wild.
(modernisation my own so original Latin is provided)

Venus

Aeneadum genetrix, hominum divumque voluptas, alma Venus.
Mother of Aeneas, delight of the gods and men, kindly Venus.
Lucretius in his poem *About the Nature of Things*

Ceres

My song is of Ceres, first to furrow the soil with the ploughshare,
First to give corn to the earth and nourishing food to mankind,
First to give laws; all things are the gift of bountiful Ceres.
Ovid, Lines 341 – 343, Book 5, *Metamorphoses*

Apollo

What may a poet ask in his prayers of You, Apollo? What can he say
as he pours a libation of new wine to You?
May, Apollo grant that I enjoy good health and a sound mind, and, I
pray, when I grow old, may He grant me a strife-free life, a clear mind
and lyre beside me with which to sing his praises.
The poet's prayer by Horace, *Odes*, 1. 31.1-4

Liber

Splendid Liber, draw near to me! With your forever mystical vine,
and your ivy bound head, carry off my sorrows, in the same manner
as you have so often used wine's healing powers to overcome the pangs
of Love!
Tibullus, *Poems* 3.6.1 – 4

Terminus

Holy Terminus, You define people and cities and nations within
their boundaries. All land would be in dispute if without You. You

seek no offence or anyone's favour; no amount of gold can corrupt
Your judgement. In good faith You preserve the legitimate claims to
rural lands.
Ovid, *Fasti* 2.658 – 62

Janus

Janus, come! The New Year is here, come and renew the sun!
Ausonius

Juno

Grant me the strength, Goddess, to whom I ask, to whom I pray;
extend your assistance to me.
Livius Andronicus

Jupiter

O Jupiter Capitolinus, to You I pray, I entreat You, who the Roman
people have named Optimus after your kindness and Maximus after
Your great power.
Cicero

Neptune

Thanks be to Neptune, my patron, who dwells in the fish-teeming salt
sea, for speeding me homeward from his sacred abode, well laden and
in good hour.
Plautus

Modern

This invocation has been channelled and created by me to
support your connection to the Capitoline Triad and for your
greatest healing and empowerment, and that of the world.
Remember that words are magic, use them wisely, with great
reverence and presence and know that your words matter, that
you are heard, seen and loved, exactly as you are and with
whatever you bring or can offer.

Holy trinity, beloved three,
Supreme of Rome!
I honour you,
I celebrate you,
And I call upon you,
With great reverence and humility,
And ask for your presence, your guidance, your wisdom
and your strength.

Hail Jupiter!
Benevolent Father of the heavens,
Mightiest, Greatest and Best.
May you please rain upon me,
Your strength, stability and wisdom.
May you help me to access the king within myself,
So that I may know when and how it is best to serve
and when and how it is best to lead.
In all my actions, words and choices may I,
Like lightning,
bring light to the stormy places,
And even when hope may just seem like thunder rumbling
in the far distance,
I trust that it *is* there and can always be found.
Remind me that there is always a will, always a way,
To stand, fight and live for justice, for restitution, for
honour, for fairness, for benevolence, for peace.
I thank you; I honour you, Id est, Id est, Id est.

Hail Juno!
Great Mother, Sovereign Queen,
Lady of light, of the heavens, the brightest star.
I call upon you now with full allowance and open enquiry,
As to all the ways in which I may heal the rifts, the
inequalities, the oppositions,

Between the masculine and the feminine,
Both within myself and in human kind.
May you bless upon us and myself, true empowerment through integration and cohesion.
Bring your light to the wounds that keep us separated from harmony, respect, compassion and equality.
May your nurturing love, forever be present in our hearts, minds, words and actions.
And, Juno Curitis, please protect me with your chariot and shield.
Please bring peace and your great guardianship and protection to all those that need you.
Bring your motherly nurturance and loving ferocity to the young, the innocent and the vulnerable, so that they may feel, and be, safe, protected, guided and guarded.
I thank you; I honour you, Id est, Id est, Id est.

Hail Minerva!
Wise and noble one,
Bestower of knowledge, great lightning bolt of inspiration,
Divine well-spring of truth and healing.
Please bless me now with the deepest knowledge of self.
Help me to understand all of the threads in my tapestry,
So that acceptance and faith may bring to light the whole picture.
Make me a channel of your wise words,
May I always speak that which supports, inspires, empowers and reassures.
Please also support me in listening with an open heart and mind,
Where no part of me is closed in judgement of what *should* be, but instead opens to what is and what could be.
This I recognise as the sweetest medicine I can give to myself and others.

Minerva, Yours is the voice that illuminates the darkness, and says,
'There is more to see here, there is more to know,
Look deeper, keep seeking,
Light a candle and let it inspire the lighting of a thousand more'.
I thank you; I honour you, Id est, Id est, Id est.

May you all be with me now,
Capitoline; Father, Mother and Wise One.
I am, I will, I trust,
I hope, I love, I bow,
and I will remember,
to be and do all that you inspire within me.
And I offer my intention to be the best I can be,
give the best I can give,
and be a foundation stone for a great legacy;
A legacy built for, and with, hope, love, truth, compassion, peace.
And so, it is and so it will be.
Id est, Id est, Id est.

Altar

You may want to create your own Roman altar. Most Roman altars were actually outside, on the portico of the Roman temple or in the central courtyard of a Roman house if they had one. However, in smaller households it may be possible that small altars were within rooms. I would advise you not to worry where your altar is, if anything, make it a central place in the house that you pass or visit often. You can create it for a specific deity, to several, or to the Roman pantheon as a whole. You could also make it seasonal, swapping and changing as you want or need.

You may also want to make an offering, light a candle or say a prayer at your altar each day, or one day of the week, perhaps with that day's associated deity e.g. Monday to Luna. Sunday to Sol.

What to Include at the Altar

Connect to your Lares (household God) and make a particular offering to them, such as food, drink or incense. Ask it, or thank it for protecting your home.

On my website you can access a meditation to connect with your household Lares. After using this you may want to draw or paint a picture of your Lares as it revealed itself, it may even have a name or favourite plant or food you can honour it with by placing that on the altar.

Imperial purple, white and gold are the symbolic colours of the Roman pantheon and could be used on altar cloths, decoration or in the colouring of items upon it, or, the colour of the clothing you wear. These colours will connect you to your inner sovereign self, and support you with working on themes of authority, discernment, choice and destiny, as well as healing and connection to the crown and solar plexus chakras.

These three serve as good base colours even if you were to create an altar for a specific deity from the pantheon.

Sacred Symbols for Ritual, and Items for Your Ceremony or Your Altar

- **SPQR Senatus Populusque Romanus** (acronym meaning: The Senate and the People of Rome), used on public monuments and legislation all over ancient Rome. Use this sign as a reminder of responsibility, legacy and that power and position should be used on behalf of the people, for humanity. See it and know that our actions should serve the greater good, and that rules and laws are meant to support, guide and facilitate healthy growth, peace, equality and justice. If they do not, they need to be reviewed and evolved with discernment, alignment with truth and communion with both the divine and the divine self (I refer to the laws that are both the personal rules we choose for ourselves and those that are used to govern.)

- For the themes of foundation, destiny, legacy, growth, fierce and nurturing love: **The She-Wolf of Rome, Goddess Lupa.** Have her statue as a singular Wolf or as the She-Wolf with the babes Romulus and Remus suckling. Both were used all over ancient Rome.

- For the themes of strength, courage, leadership, perspective and expansion chose the symbol of the **Eagle of Jupiter.** It is also a symbol of the ancient Roman empire and people. Use it when you feel you need or want to embody your sovereign self, that is wise and discerning and, or, to connect to your highest self and wisdom.

- **For invoking the energy, essence or archetype of Emperor** use a laurel or oak wreath, Pearls (a favourite of Julius Ceaser who collected them) or The Imperium/ Fasces. These symbols remind you that you and you alone are responsible for yourself. Act with integrity, take responsibility for your actions, thoughts and words and embody your unique purpose.

You may also want to have these additional items:

- **Geese** – Image or statue of a goose/geese or the feathers of a goose (sustainably and ethically sourced). For protection and guardianship, as the sacred bird of Juno.
- **Candle** – Vesta's flame. For longevity and hope. Also, red, yellow or orange candles for Vesta or purple, white or gold candles for the symbolic colours of Imperial Rome.

- **Roman Numerals** – You could use numerals rather than numbers. You could choose a number that is meaningful for you, such as your birth day and write it, paint it, scribe it.

- **Olives, Olive essence or olive branch** – Olive symbolically holds the keys and codes of emperor and kingship and will connect you to your own inner authority and will remind you of the wisdom that is held within so that you use it as a tool for sacred service.

- **Roman Coins** – Perhaps will a particular deity or emperor depicted if you have a preference.

- **Circle** – Symbolic of the boundary wall, both literal, symbolic and protective, created by Romulus and affirmed and built by later Romans.

- **Snake** – In Roman art the snake was a symbol for the soul (genius). They were considered a good omen and were also associated with healing, fertility and rebirth.

- **Marble** – You may want statues of your chosen deities in marble or a pillar of marble to symbolise the temple or to mark sacred space.

- **Water** – To symbolise the River Tiber or specific water deities of Rome, such as Jupiter, Neptune, Salus, Salacia and Juventas.

Offerings

Mol Salsa

Mola Salsa ("salted mill/millstone") was a mixture of coarse-ground toasted flour and salt prepared by the Vestal Virgins for the festivals of Vestalia, Lupercalia and at the Epulum Iovis. Ritual was also important during the making of Mol Salsa and the Vestal Virgins made the cakes using water from a sacred spring. The water must not have touched the earth between the spring and the temple of Vesta. It is often named 'salted-spelt' in the ancient texts and was used for rituals, alongside wine.

Other food stuff

It was rare too fast for religious purposes in ancient Rome and feasting was a frequent part of religious celebrations and food a common offering. The following fruits and associated trees, leaves, flowers or produce had significance for the ancient Romans and were all used in religious contexts as offerings; bread, cakes, grains, figs, olives, citrus, pomegranates, dates.

Spices which in Latin *specia*, means 'special', were also used as offering. Common spices were basil, ginger, cumin, cinnamon, black pepper, chilli, cumin, garlic, parsley and celery salt. You can use the spices for ceremonial mulled wine, as well as in or as food offerings.

Rosemary

An important herb to the Romans was rosemary, or rome's-mary as I like to call it. It grew wild on the hills of ancient Italy and was used in cooking and the household, as well as in ritual and offerings. The blue blossoms led it to be called *ros marinus*, dew of the sea. It is an ancient symbol of love and remembrance and was used in both marriages and funeral rites of ancient Rome.

In his book *Natural History*, Pliny the Elder, ancient Roman author, naturalist, and natural philosopher notes the many healing benefits of Rosemary and offers an example of how the Romans held rosemary as an all healer and sacred herb[19].

Rosemary is also connected to many Roman deities; Minerva, Lupa, Neptune, Venus and Juno, and was used as an offering to them.

There are many ways you can use rosemary; as tea, as incense, as offering, as altar decoration, cleansing stick, as essential oil in massage or anointing oil, charms, crowns, amulets, flower essence and in ceremonial food.

Rosemary Flower Essence is one of the great protector essences. Rosemary Flower Essence helps with your journey of embodiment, integrating the disparate parts of Self into a cohesive Wholeness.

I also like to use it as an anointing oil for my throat and head and if you choose to do so as well, I would recommend diluting 3–5 drops essential oil per 1 teaspoon carrier oil (Use 1 drop essential oil per 1 tablespoon carrier oil for animals or children). As an essential oil rosemary holds the wisdom and healing of remembrance and clarity and also supports healthy mental, emotional and physical energy levels.

You can also grow rosemary in your garden for use or add to a Roman themed garden feature or area.

I have created a free Rosemary Flower Essence Journey and Anointing Ritual that you can enjoy and access via my website for free.

Laurel

For the ancient Romans, laurel (bay laurel) represented victory and achievement. The horseshoe shaped laurel wreath was a symbol of victory in that it was used for crowning a successful commander during a triumph. The laurel wreath worn on the head was also believed to provide and represent mental strength. Laurel was also sacred to the emperor. Analysis of remaining roots next to Augustus's Parthian Arch in the Roman Forum have revealed that it was flanked by living laurel trees.

The Romans also considered it a powerful protection against evil and disease. The Laurel crown was worn by Apollo, the god of disease and cure and it is his sacred tree. Tradition says that Emperor Tiberius was noted for wearing a laurel crown for protection during thunderstorms as he was so afraid of them. Emperor Nero apparently also sat under a laurel tree during an outbreak of plague in the city of Rome. He sat there to protect himself against the disease and received all of his petitioners there until the danger passed.

As a Flower Essence, Laurel holds the healing codes of resourcefulness. It invites you to hold your vision, get organised and bring your plans into manifestation. Laurel flower essence helps you to plan, structure, organise and direct your thoughts and actions in line with your deepest and highest intention. Use it for embracing success and acknowledging and healing fears of failure. Take two drops in ceremony or three drops three times daily.

You can use Bay Laurel Essential Oil to anoint the crown, hands and feet, especially during connection, ceremony or meditation with Apollo, Jupiter, Mars, Victoria or Fortuna. The essential oil can support you in finding ease.

You can connect to Laurel by making your own laurel crown, to wear when working with or embodying the energy of Emperor. It was also traditional in ancient Rome to have a bay laurel tree at the doorways or windows to your home, to stop evil from entering and you can continue this practice. You can also burn dried laurel bay leaves as incense, or place the leaves upon your altar as protection.

If you can't get hold of Laurel use oak leaves instead. In ancient Rome there was an oak leafed 'civic crown' which was an honorary crown, known as *corona ciuica*. Such a crown was presented to Emperor Augustus for saving the life of Roman citizens in 27 BCE. One was also hung above his door of his palace on the Palatine. It was thought to offer protection as the mighty oak tree symbolises protective strength and guardianship. As with Laurel, Oak Tree Essence can be used in the same way to adorn or anoint the ground for protection or to honour, commemorate or symbolise a protector or act of protection. Beech leaves were also used for ceremonies with Ceres and a beech leaf crown was worn during her festival of Cerialia.

Other Plants, Flowers and Herbs.

All Flowers were considered the manifestation and creation of Goddess Flora. However, some were also connected to other deities.

- Roses were particularly associated with the commemoration of the dead. Tombs and graves were garlanded with Roses during the Dies Rosationis. Rosalia, or 'a festival of Roses', refers to the use of Roses in the commemoration of certain events.
- The cornel tree was connected to the mythology of Romulus. From a sacred cornel tree on Aventine Hill, he crafted a spear which he hurled into the ground to test his strength. It sank so deep into the ground that none could pull it out. Many tried to pull the spear from the ground but could not. Instead, it rooted, sprouted and became a mighty and sacred tree that Romulus venerated. After him it continued to be held sacred, was tended and a wall of sanctified space was built around it.
- The most common plant motif used in Roman architecture, such as columns and reliefs, what that of the Acanthus. It symbolised enduring life.
- Flowers of symbolic significance found on Roman coins include hellebore, lily, wild celery, opium poppy and pomegranate.
- Common herbs cultivated and used in Roman times for various uses; Herb Robert, Pot Marigold, common rue, lavender, hyssop, dill, bay, fennel, sage, rosemary, garlic, mint, feverfew, borage, coriander, lovage, sweet cicely, basil, oregano, parsley, thyme, lemon balm, hyssop, lavender, fenugreek, henbane, centaury, St John's Wort, plantain, and wormwood.

- We know from letters of the ancient Romans, such as Pliny the Younger and the records of Pliny the Elder, in *Historia Naturalis*, that many villas had mulberry's, apple, citrus, pomegranate, medlar, cypress, myrtle, vine and fig trees in their gardens, along with flowers such as periwinkle, narcissi, roses, lilies, rosemary, acanthus, violet, poppy, mallow, anemone, peony, ivy and iris. Olive was the most cultivated and grown tree in the Roman empire. All of these plants could be used to create a Roman style garden, or for offering or indoor and outdoor altar decoration.

Flowers are a great biodegradable offering that also connects us to our ancestors through continued use. Consider growing Roman herbs and flowers in your own garden, allotment or window ledge, rather than buying them and for the most eco-friendly method use Flower Essence formulas.

Fruit

Fruit was considered the manifestation and creation of Goddess Pomona, Goddess of the orchard, gardens and fruit trees. These are the common fruits that were available to the ancient Romans, that could be used in ritual, ceremony, as offerings and for consumption in a feast or picnic (if you were say to celebrate a Roman festival with a gathering or meal).

Grape, fig, lemon, walnut, hops, crab apple, medlar, mulberry, cherry, plum, damson, peach, blackberry, pear, raspberry, pomegranate, apricot.

Some of these fruits and trees were cultivated and others were gathered wild. You could also use the juice of some of these fruits, to consume or as libation.

Wine

Use wine as a libation, red, rose or white. Red was the wine that was commonly used by general Roman citizens as it was more readily available. White wine was only used and consumed by the upper classes but either is fine for an offering. The colour can be symbolic of the red of human or animal blood, the white of divine blood. Red and white wine together can represent the masculine and feminine and divine union, such as the union of Jupiter and Juno.

Have a glass of wine on your altar or use it to pour as a libation on the ground. You can offer a small amount as a daily gratitude or choose to always offer half of what you use in ceremony, ritual or even when you are drinking it for your own pleasure. You can also use it to anoint your forehead as was done by the ancient Romans in ceremony. The ancient Romans believed that drunkenness offended both the gods and the ancestors.

Wine was particularly connected to the God Baccus, the God of Wine and to the God Liber.

Grape juice or honeyed water is great to use as an alternative.

Incense

Cinnamon was used as an incense by the Romans at funerals. Saffron, Myrrh and Frankincense incense were also frequently used by the Romans. Rosemary leaves were also burnt.

Crystals and Minerals

Carnelian, Aventurine, Citrine, Garnet and Amethyst are great crystals for empowerment, for expansion, and for reaching your highest potential. Use Gold for connecting to or symbolising kingship and sovereignty. To connect with or to honour the Etruscans and early Rome, use Bronze. To connect with or to honour the Romans, use white marble.

Activities to Connect with the Roman Pantheon

Here are some introductory ideas for activities to begin establishing a relationship with the Roman pantheon. All of these activities are child-friendly!

- Create or decorate your own Toga, God or Goddess themed. Rome was known by many of its allies and enemies as 'the race that wears the toga'. The word toga derives from the verb *tegere*, meaning to cover. The toga was considered your 'best dress' and worn during ceremonies, rituals and important occasions. In a similar way the *palla* was a veil worn over the head or shoulders by a Roman woman. Your own toga or palla can be worn as ceremonial wear during ritual, ceremony, meditation (doubling up as a great sacred blanket). You may want to have it white as per the ordinary Roman toga, or have it a symbolic colour that matches your chosen deity/deities, such as red for Mars or Bellona, gold for Fortuna, Juno or Ceres, black for Pluto/Orcus and Tellus Mater, blue for Minerva or Neptune, purple for Roma or Jupiter, orange for Vesta, grey for Romulus, green for Venus. A toga is typically made of large piece of woollen cloth and was circular in shape, then folded in half and draped over and under the shoulder. It can be a powerful mantle, shamanic cape, ceremonial robe that can connect you to the Roman pantheon and the Romans of the past.
- Make a mosaic of your favourite God or Goddess for your altar or as a devotional ritual. The Romans used stone, glass, pebbles, marbles, terracotta and tiles to create their mosaics, which often depicted scenes from mythology and legend. You don't have to use fragments of stone and glass like the Romans, although you can! Instead, you could use card, magazine fragments, crystals, clay, recycled jewellery, beads, cloth/fabric, even things like

dried pasta! You could also paint in a mosaic style. Draw a rough sketch first, perhaps using an original Roman picture or mosaic as inspiration, then collect your *tesserae* (cubes) and plan the colours, layout and placement before creating your mosaic.

- Make a Laurel Crown with Jupiter and Juno using bay laurel leaves. Call in or become aware of Jupiter and Juno's presence. Weave and twist bay leaves and their stalks into a horseshoes shaped crown, attaching them to wire, ribbon or string already measured to fit around your head. You can also paint the bay leaves in gold paint if you wish. Accompany this activity by journalling or considering what sovereignty means to you.

Get a piece of paper or journal and answer, and reflect on, the following questions:

1. What does sovereignty mean and encompass for me? What feelings, fears, hope, judgements, desires or wounds does the word or idea bring up?
2. How is my relationship with trust? Including; trust of self, trust of your body, trust of life, trust of the divine, trust of others? *Write on this in detail.*
3. In what ways do I limit or hold back my true self, or make myself small? What conditions or judgements have I created, chosen or inherited that prevent me from expanding into my full potential?
4. Who am I essentially, when I am not the judgements and conditions placed upon me?
5. What does my most authentic self, look, feel, act and speak like?
6. What makes me my highest self?
7. What truly and honestly brings me joy and a feeling of ease to my soul and body?

8. What does it mean to respect myself? How would my life and self, look and feel if I acted with devotion, compassion and respect for myself and my truth?
9. How am I divine?
10. List twenty blessings that are you in your life right now.

The Laurel crown will symbolise or contain the energy of your answers, intentions and insights.

- Set up a household or garden altar to your home's Lares. The household shrine was called the lararium and was usually situated in the atrium, the centre of the house. Statues of metal, terracotta or stone were often placed in Roman gardens.

1. Use my audio guided meditation to first connect to your household Lares and to ask for their continued presence and blessings on your house.
2. Designate a particular area that will become sanctified space for your altar. For the Romans this was normally in the courtyard at the centre of the house so that it would be passed frequently. A good place would be in or near your kitchen, a place where you visit frequently and can offer a portion of every meal/drink. Make daily or weekly offerings at your designated sacred space and perhaps celebrate or hold a ritual or banquet for the birthday of your house, or annually in honour of the day you moved there, or first connected with your Lares.
3. Work in communion with your Lares, consult them on household decisions, for example, if you are considering redecorating or buildings works. Ask for their help or support when things come up such as leaks or unwanted guests.

Aqueduct Meditation

This meditation is inspired by the Roman engineering innovation of managing the flow of water along aqueducts and canals. They channelled water from fresh springs, streams and lakes into the cities. The first aqueduct was built in Rome in the 2nd century BCE and they were essential for town life, bringing water from natural sources into the towns and cities. Likewise, this meditation for your rejuvenation and nourishment.

Before you begin make sure you are in a comfortable position where you won't be disturbed. You may want to light a candle, invite into your space and ritual a Roman water deity such as Neptune or Juventas. You may also want to have water present on your altar, or use this practice in the shower or bath, near a waterfall or river, though this isn't necessary.

It is also a great meditation to either start or end your start, to cleanse yourself energetically or emotionally. However, it is also ok to just use it for relaxation! Read it a few times to memorize or on my website you will find an audio recording of this meditation that I have made for you to listen to.

Begin by placing your hands upon your body, somewhere that feels supportive to you, and close your eyes. Take seven deep breaths, each time gradually deepening and lengthening your breath. Then with each breath in, imagine water coming up as a spring from deep in the earth. See in your mind's eye fresh water bubbling up from a spring high in the mountains. The spring is a source of the most nourishing, cleansing water, pure and sparkling in the sunlight. Follow the journey of the water from the spring, as it gradually becomes a brook, a waterfall, a water flow that enters an aqueduct on the mountain. You hear and see it running down the channel of the aqueduct, leaving the mountain, travelling through fields, over rivers and forests. The flow is gentle, consistent, soothing. The aqueduct finally comes to the place where you are, channelling down to a circular basin that sits just above your head. Through an opening in this basin, allow the sacred waters from above to flow down through your body. Be the vessel ready to receive; opening, surrendering, relaxing. See and feel fresh, clear, sparkling water pouring or trickling down over your head, and then through the valleys, gorges and channels of your body. With each breath out send the water through your body, refreshing and revitalising. The water clears away any debris or stagnancy. It brings ease and clarity to your whole body and mind. With each breath the water continues to ripple through you. Is there anywhere in particular you want to direct it? Create a channel to anywhere in your body or mind that needs nourishment and the cleansing of this sacred water. Perhaps some areas within you need more than others. Visualise the water flowing to those places like water reaching a fountain and then overflowing into that place.

Receive as much as you need, until you your mind, body and soul feel hydrated!

When you are ready just see the flow of the water change from running water to a trickle, and finally to a drip. The basin closes and the water flow stops.

Thank the water and let it know that you are done.

When you are ready, breathe deeply and stretch your body before opening your eyes and returning to your day.

Conclusion

Every new beginning comes from some other beginning's end.

Marcus Annaeus Seneca, known as Seneca the Elder (54 BCE – 39 CE)

I hope you have enjoyed this short introduction to the religion of ancient Rome and its pantheon of gods and goddesses. Use this book a starting point to further explore areas or subjects that particularly drew your interest. You will find primary and secondary resources in my bibliography that offer pathways for further research. It contains all of the books that contributed to the background research for this book.

Perhaps you could even take this book with you on your next visit to Rome or a Roman historical site, as a compliment to all your maps and guidebooks. If you do, don't forget to take a photograph and tag me on social media, I would love to see your adventures!

I also have more resources for you to support and continue your journey.

You can find on my website extra free resources:

- An audio recording of the Triad invocation, so that you can join along with me in a short ritual.
- A free Rosemary Flower Essence journey and optional short anointing ritual.
- Short videos on 'How to Connect with the Roman gods and goddesses', my YouTube series of my top three tips and tools for connecting to specific Roman deities.

- A fun quiz for you to enjoy; 'Which Roman deity is your guide' to discover which Roman god or goddess would be your best ally right now.
- An audio recording of my aqueduct meditation.
- Various meditations with the She-Wolf of Rome, Goddess Lupa.

I also provide an online bundle which includes:

- An audio journey meditation to meet your personal Genius.
- Connect to your household Lares and Terminus, God of boundaries, through ritual and invocation.
- A guided meditation to experience a journey with Goddess Vesta or God Janus, to receive their wisdom and healing.

Find them all by visiting www.wolfwomanrising.com

I hope all of this supports and nourishes you! Thanks for reading and many blessings, Rachel

Connect with Rachel on social media:
Facebook @wolfwomanrising
Instagram @wolfwomanrisingofficial
You Tube @wolfwomanrising

Glossary of Terms

Aborigines – A term used by ancient Roman writers to describe the original people of Italy, that were not part of an invading or immigrant cultures or people.

Aedes – A name used to designate to dwelling place or house of a god, such as a building or shrine. For example, the regimental shrine at the centre of a legion's headquarters.

Aedile (Pl. Aediles) – Magistrates responsible for the organisation of public buildings, games and the supply and distribution of corn.

Augury – The divining of the future by observation of natural phenomena, in particular the behaviour of birds and animals. A priest who practiced augury was called an augur.

Capitoline Triad – The three principal deities of ancient Rome: Jupiter, Juno and Minerva.

Curio – The priest that was in charge of the sacrifices in each of the curiae (the districts that the Roman people were divided into).

Damnatio memoriae – The eradication of the memory of a person after death, for example, by the removal of their name and statues from all public and private places.

Di Consentes – Comprised the twelve major Roman deities of the Roman pantheon.

Di Selecti – Were considered the main twenty deities of ancient Roman religion.

Etruscans – The people and culture that occupied the area of Etruria before the Roman conquest.

Evander – Son of the Goddess Carmenta and an arcadian hero who was identified with the worship of the God Faunus and was considered the first settler of the area that became Rome.

Fasti – Ancient Roman calendars that recorded religious and official events and observances.

Flamines – A special priest that was devoted to a single deity.

Genius/ Genii – Guardian spirit, essence or soul. In reference to the divinity contained in all things. Every person and thing have a genius. Genii was often depicted as a snake.

Genius loci – A guardian spirit that was attending a particular place.

Hepatoscopy – Divination through means of dissecting and examining an animal liver. Believed to be Etruscan in origin.

Ides – The thirteenth day of the month, with the exception of March, May, July and October when the Ides was the fifteenth of the month.

Kalends – First day of the month, such as 'The kalends of June'. The first of the month was considered a particularly sacred day and often associated with a deity or festival.

Lararia – The household shrine, where the Lares or household deities were honoured.

Lares – Household or domestic spirit that was a guardian of that place.

Latins – The people that populated Latium before the Roman conquest, an area south of Rome.

Libation – An offering or drink poured to a deity, usually on the ground or altar.

Manes – A term used for the collective dead or souls of the dead.

Materfamilias – The female head of a family or household.

Mausolea – A structure/building built of stone to housing the dead.

Munera – Duty or obligations that were required to be made, such as in the case of honouring the dead with games and feasts.

Numen – The divine quality of something.

Paterfamilias – The male head of a family or household.

Pietas – The duty of a Roman towards his country, his gods and his family, both alive and dead.

Pontifax Maximus – Meaning highest priest.

Portico – A porch leading to the entrance of a sacred building, such as the Portico of the Consenting Gods.

Rex Sacrorum – When the Roman monarchy was abolished the rex sacrorum was a role established to substitute for the king. He was a senior priest who performed the traditional sacrificial and religious duties previously conducted by a king.

Rubican – The river that marked the border between the territory of Rome and the province of Rome.

Sacer/Sacra (feminine) – Something consecrated to a deity, or itself made divine, such as the Sacred Way (Sacra Via) through Rome.

Sacrarium – Shrine to a deity.

Tribute – A payment made by people to a ruler or conqueror.

Triumph – The parade into Rome of a victorious general.

Uates – A speaker, singer, orator or prophet inspired by the divine, that shared or channelled divine wisdom and prophecy. Sometimes equated with bard or poet.

Maps of Ancient Rome

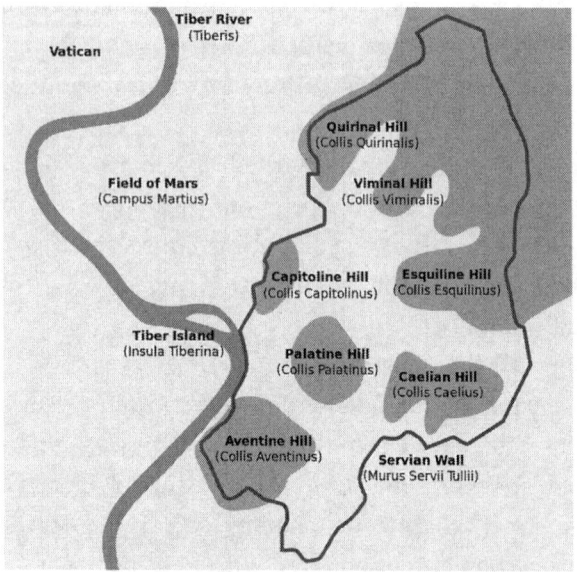

Map of Ancient Rome and her seven hills.

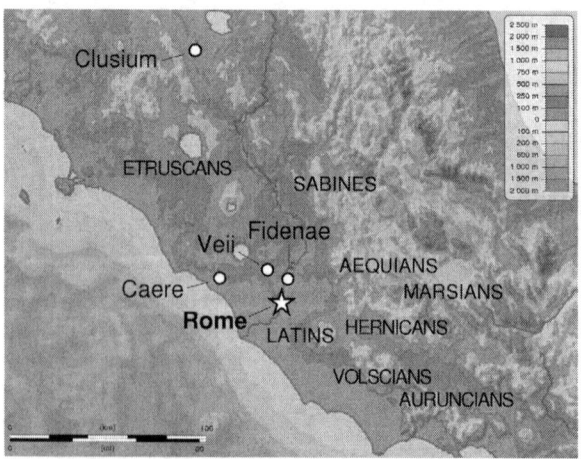

Map of the tribes of central western Italy at the time of Rome's
foundation.

Endnotes

1. This was a date that was traditionally agreed on by consuls of the Roman Republic and then written down for prosperity by Marcus Terentius Varro, considered the greatest Roman scholar, as part of his compilation of the Varronian chronology. He objective was to determine an exact year-by-year timeline of Roman history up to his time by tracing back through significant events and the reigns of the Kings of Rome.
2. Roman plaque from a Roman tomb, 3rd Century.
3. Dionysius of Halicarnassus tells us that the Etruscans and Villanovans were aborigines of Italy, though there was some speculation that they may have been immigrants from Sardinia in very ancient times beyond remembrance. He also shares that it was believed that the Sabines came from Umbria in northern Italy and stole land around Rome from the aborigines of Italy in the 10th century BCE. He believed the Umbrians themselves were descendants of the Spartans, however, historians believe this was an attempt to connect Roman history to that of the Greeks.
4. See Ovid, *Fasti*, Book 2, Lines 289 -303.
5. Brother and sister referring to Apollo the sun and Diana the moon.
6. Vows or prayers, however, never made to the emperor's genius as they were to the deities and it was the deities that were always ultimately turned to in times of danger or illness.
7. See Wiseman's translation of Ovid's *Fasti*.
8. In some parts of the empire, especially in Northern Europe there was a belief in the realm of the dead being the other

side of the great river, Oceanus. It was believed that Oceanus surrounded the earth and so one had to travel across the water via boat, dolphins or other nautical devices to reach the afterlife.

9. I share much more about the connection between Wolves and the Roman and Etruscan afterlife and life, death and rebirth traditions in my book *Lupa. She Wolf of Rome, Mother of Destiny*.

10. See Ovid, *Fasti*, Book 2. 21st February.

11. Ten months was considered the appropriate time for a year of mourning as this is the time length of pregnancy and so for new life to be formed. This time of mourning began at the funeral.

12. Whereas adult protective amulets tended towards images of a phallus, gorgons head or the mano fico gesture.

13. I suggest in my book, *Lupa*, that the use of Wolf fat was a religious reference to Lupa, the Mother She-Wolf who protected the founders of Rome, Romulus and Remus, in the hopes that the Great Wolf of Rome would likewise protect the home. It offers an interesting and symbolic link between the Genius Materfamilias of Rome as the She-Wolf Goddess, both whom are called upon to protect children and home.

14. See Ovid, *Fasti*, Book 4, April 19th.

15. Fasting was very rare in Roman times and the idea of fasting was very much seen as Greek and therefore uncouth.

16. The conception and birth of Mars was written down by Ovid in his work *Fasti*.

17. Ovid is an example of the Roman belief in Saturn as the original ruler or period of existence. In *Fasti* he has Saturn arriving in Rome at the beginning of time. His rule in Rome, according to Ovid, was followed by Janus and then later the hero Evander.

18. The name Latium was thought to be derived from Saturn himself, the 'God in Hiding; with *Latere* being Latin for hiding or being unobserved and refers to Saturn hiding from Jupiter.

19. He shares that Rosemary has eighteen remedies. *The Natural History*. Pliny the Elder, Chapter 59, 62 and 64.

Bibliography

Primary Sources

Apuleius., *The Golden Ass.* Patrick Gerard Walsh (trans.) (Oxford, Oxford University Press. 1999).

Aurelias, Marcus., *Meditations.* Martin Hammond (ed. And trans.) (London, Penguin Classics, 2006).

Cato, Marcus Porcius., *On Farming.* Dalby, A., (ed. And trans.) (Sheffield, Prospect Books, 1998).

Catullus., *Poems of love and hate.* Balmer, J. (trans.) (Northumberland, Bloodaxe Books, 2004).

Cicero, M., *On Old Age. On Friendship. On Divination.* W.A Falconer (ed. And trans.) (London, Penguin Books, 1989).

Cicero, M., *The Nature of Gods.* P.G Walsh (ed. And trans.) (Oxford, Oxford University Press, 2008).

Columella., *De Re Rustica. On Agriculture. Vo. 1* H. b. Ash (ed. And trans.) (London, Heinemann, 1942).

Dionysius of Halicarnassus., *The Roman Antiquities.* Aeterna Press (trans.) (Indonesia, Lighthouse Publishing, 2015).

Ennius, Quintus, *The Annals.* Edith Mary Steuart (ed. And trans.) (Cambridge, Cambridge University Press, 2014).

Gellius, Aulus. *Attic Nights, Books 1-5.* Rolfe, J.C. (ed. And trans.) (London, Harvard University Press, 1989)

Horace., *The Complete Odes and Epodes.* David West. (ed. And trans) (Oxford, Oxford University Press).

Juvenal., *Juvenal Satires Book I,* Braud, Susana (trans.) (Cambridge, University of Cambridge Press. 1996).

Livy, T., *The Early History of Rome: Books I-V of the History of Rome from its foundations.* R.M. Ogilvie (trans.) (London, Penguin Classics, 2008).

Lucretius., *On the Nature of Things.* Stallings, Alicia (trans.) (Oxford, Penguin Classics, 2008).

Manilius., *Astronomica.* Goold, G.P. (trans.) (London, Heinemann, 1977).

Martial., *Epigrams.* Garry Willis (ed. And trans.) (New York, Penguin Random House, 2008).

Maximus, Valerius., *Memorable Doings and Sayings. Volume 1: Books 1-5.* Shackleton Bailey (trans.) (London, Harvard University Press, 2000).

Ovid., *Fasti.* A Wiseman & P. Wiseman (trans.) (Oxford, Oxford University Press, 2011).

Ovid., *Metamorphoses.* D Raeburn (trans.) (London, Penguin Classics, 2004).

Petronius., *The Satyricon.* Burman, Pieter. (trans.) (Jiahu Books, 2013).

Pliny the Elder., *Natural History.* J. Healey (trans.) (London, Penguin Books, 1991).

Pliny the Younger., *The letters of the Younger Pliny.* Radice, Betty (trans) (Harmondsworth: Penguin Books, 1970).

Plutarch., *Essays.*, R. Waterfield. (trans.) (London, Penguin Books, 1991).

Plutarch., *Fall of the Roman Republic: Six Lives.* R. Seager (trans.) (London, Penguin Books, 2006).

Plutarch., *The Rise of Rome. Twelve Lives.* Scott-Kilvert, I., Tatum, J., & Pelling. C. (trans) (London, Penguin Books, 2013).

Propertius., *The Poems.* Lee, G., (trans) (Oxford, Oxford World Classics for Oxford University Press, 2009).

Seneca., *Letters from a Stoic.* Campbell, Robin (trans.) (London, Penguin Books, 2004).

Suetonius., *The Twelve Ceasars.* Graves, R., (trans.) (London, Penguin Books, 2007).

Tacitus., *The Annals of Imperial Rome.* Grant, M. (trans.) (London, Penguin Books, 2003).

Tacitus., *The Agricola and the Germanica.* Mattingly, H (trans) (Harmondsworth Press. Penguin books 1970).

Tacitus., The Histories. Wellesley, K., (trans.) (London, Penguin Classics, 2009).

Varro., *On the Latin Language*. Kent, R.G. (trans.) (London, Loeb Classical of Heinemann Library, 1989).

Virgil., *The Aeneid*. West, D. (trans) (London. Penguin Classics, 2003).

Virgil., *The Pastoral Poems*. Rieu, E.V. (trans) (Middlesex, Penguin Classics, 1972).

Secondary Sources

Beard, M. *Emperor of Rome. Ruling the Ancient Roman World* (London, Profile Books, 2023).

Beard, M., and North, J. (eds) *Pagan Priests. Religion and Power in the Ancient World* (London, Duckworth, 1990).

Bédoyère, Guy De La. *Gladius. Living, Fighting and Dying in the Roan Army*. (London, Abacus, 2020).

Billington, S and Green, M. (eds.) *The concept of the Goddess* (London, Routledge, 2002).

Boardman, J, Griffin, J., and Murray, O. (eds) *The Oxford History of the Classical World* (Oxford, Oxford University Press, 1991).

Bonner, S. F. *Education in Ancient Rome* (Oxon, Routledge, 2012).

Bradley, K. *Discovering the Roman Family. Studies in Roman Social History* (Oxford, Oxford University Press, 1991).

Bradley, K. *Slaves and Masters in the Roman Empire: A study in social control* (New York, Oxford University Press, 1997).

Bremmer, J. N., and Horsfall, N. M. *Roman Myth and Mythography*. (London, University of London Institute of Classical studies, 1987).

Cornell, T. J. and Dodge, H (eds.) *Ancient Rome. The Archaeology of the Eternal City*. (Oxford, Oxford University School of Archaeology, 1995).

Cornell, T. J. *The beginnings of Rome: Italy and Rome from the Bronze Age to the Punic Wars* (c.100 -264 BCE) (London, Routledge, 1995).

Dixon, Suzanne. *The Roman Mother*. (Oxon, Routledge, 2014).

Dudley, D. R. *The World of Tacitus*. (London, Secker and Warburg, 1968).

Edwards, Catherine. *The Politics of Immortality in Ancient Rome* (Cambridge, Cambridge University Press, 1993).

Fantham, E. *Latin Poets and Italian Gods* (Toronto. University of Toronto Press, 2009).

Ferres, I. *Cave Canem. Animals and Roman Society*. (Stroud. Amberley, 2018).

Fisher, J. *The Annals of Quintus Ennius* (Baltimore, Johns Hopkins University Press, 2014).

Forsythe, H. I. *A critical History of Early Rome: From prehistory to the First Punic War* (New York, Berkley, 2005).

Gardner, J. F. *Women in Roman Law and Society* (Kent, Croom Helm, 1986).

Gardner, J. F., & Wiedemann, T. *The Roman Household. A Sourcebook*. (London, Routledge, 2002).

Holloway, R. *The Archaeology of Early Rome and Latium* (Abingdon, Routledge, 1996).

Jackson, R. *Doctors and Diseases in the Roman Empire* (London, A. & C. Black, 1988).

Jennings, Anne. *Roman Gardens*. (London, English Heritage, 2006).

Kraemer, Ross, S. *Women's Religions in the Greco-Roman World. A Sourcebook*. (New York, Oxford University Press, 2004).

Marshall, E. and Hope, V. *Death and Disease in the Ancient City* (Abingdon, Routledge, 2000).

McGinn, T. *Prostitution, Sexuality and Law in Ancient Rome*. (Oxford, Oxford University Press, 1998).

Meijer, P. A. *Stoic Theology: Proofs for the existence of the cosmic gods and the traditional gods* (Vredenburg, Euburon Academic Publishers, 2007).

Reece, R. (ed). *Burial in the Roman World*. (London, Council for British Archaeology, 1977).

Roman, M., & Roman, Luke. *Aphrodite to Zeus: An encyclopaedia of Greek and Roman Mythology*. (New York, Checkmark Books. 2011).

Roller, L. E. *In Search of God The Mother. The Cult of Anatolian Cybele*. (London, University of California Press, 1999).

Scullard, H. H. *Festivals and Ceremonies of the Roman Republic*. (London, Thames and Hudson, 1981).

Spivey, N. *Etruscan Art*. (London, Thames and Hudson, 1997).

Staples, A. *From Good Goddess to Vestal Virgins: Sex and Category in Roman Religions*. (London and New York, Routledge, 1998).

Sutherland, C.H.V. *Roman Coins*. (London, Barrie and Jenkins, 1974).

Thomson de Grummond, Nancy. *Etruscan myth, sacred history, and legend*. (University of Pennsylvania Museum of Archaeology and Anthropology, University of Pennsylvania Press. 2006).

Toynbee, J. M. C. *Death and Burial in the Roman World*. (London, Thames and Hudson, 1971).

Wellard, James. *The Search for the Etruscans*. (Tennessee, Thomas Nelson and Sons Ltd. 1973).

Wildfang, Robin Lorsch. *Rome's Vestal Virgins: A Study of Rome's Vestal Priestesses in the Late Republic and Early Empire*. (Abingdon, Routledge, 2006).

Wiseman, T. P. *Roman Drama and Roman History* (Exeter, University of Exter Press, 1998).

Zanker, P. *The Power of Images in the Age of Augustus*, trans. A. Shapiro (Michigan University Press, 1988).

MOON BOOKS
PAGANISM & SHAMANISM

What is Paganism? A religion, a spirituality, an alternative
belief system, nature worship? You can find support for
all these definitions (and many more) in dictionaries,
encyclopaedias, and text books of religion, but subscribe to
any one and the truth will evade you. Above all Paganism is
a creative pursuit, an encounter with reality, an exploration
of meaning and an expression of the soul. Druids, Heathens,
Wiccans and others, all contribute their insights and literary
riches to the Pagan tradition. Moon Books invites you
to begin or to deepen your own encounter,
right here, right now.

If you have enjoyed this book, why not tell other readers by
posting a review on your preferred book site.

Readers of ebooks can buy or view any of these bestsellers by clicking on the live link in the title. Most titles are published in paperback and as an ebook. Paperbacks are available in traditional bookshops. Both print and ebook formats are available online.

Find more titles and sign up to our readers' newsletter
www.collectiveinkbooks.com/paganism

For video content, author interviews and more, please subscribe to our YouTube channel.

MoonBooksPublishing

Follow us on social media for book news, promotions and more:

Facebook: Moon Books

Instagram: @MoonBooksCI

X: @MoonBooksCI

TikTok: @MoonBooksCI

Printed and bound by CPI Group (UK) Ltd, Croydon, CR0 4YY

13/11/2025

01997193-0004